T0312033

Strategy Discovery

Personal, useful, actionable and grounded in research, this book will shift your thinking from "strategy development" to "strategy discovery" to enable you to deal with today's business challenges, engage your staff and boost your business performance.

Management teams and boards are facing disruption on all sides, from morphing customer preferences to the COVID pandemic to climate change. At the same time they are floundering in strategy confusion with too many concepts and not enough clarity. In this book, strategy expert and regular *Harvard Business Review* author Graham Kenny releases managers and directors from their strategy haze. His simple and effective framework allows managers to navigate the current maze of ideas and approaches and maximize their competitive advantage. Kenny's readable style is equally effective: each chapter begins with an engaging story, then builds on this with cases, client examples, sidebars and more, ending with a series of action points to provide a pathway to success.

CEOs, senior-level and middle managers across all functions and sectors, including private, public and not-for-profit organizations, who discuss and set strategy for their organization or business unit will appreciate the articulated framework, illustrative anecdotes and positive encouragement this book offers.

Graham Kenny is an internationally recognized expert in strategy and performance measurement. He writes regularly for the *Harvard Business Review*, has written more than 70 articles for international academic journals and has authored five books. He is passionate about helping boards, executives and managers lead successful organizations in the public, private and not-for-profit sectors. He has been a professor of management in universities in the US and Canada.

Strategy Discovery

Achieving Business Resilience, Engagement and Performance

Graham Kenny

Routledge
Taylor & Francis Group
NEW YORK AND LONDON

Designed cover image: © Getty images

First published 2024
by Routledge
605 Third Avenue, New York, NY 10158

and by Routledge
4 Park Square, Milton Park, Abingdon, Oxon, OX14 4RN

Routledge is an imprint of the Taylor & Francis Group, an informa business

© 2024 Graham Kenny

Library of Congress Cataloging-in-Publication Data
Names: Kenny, Graham, author.
Title: Strategy discovery : achieving business resilience, engagement, and performance / Graham Kenny.
Description: New York, NY : Routledge, 2024. | Includes bibliographical references and index.
Identifiers: LCCN 2023015741 (print) | LCCN 2023015742 (ebook) | ISBN 9781032496832 (hardback) | ISBN 9781032496528 (paperback) | ISBN 9781003394976 (ebook)
Subjects: LCSH: Strategic planning. | Organizational change. | Organizational resilience.
Classification: LCC HD30.28 .K458 2024 (print) | LCC HD30.28 (ebook) | DDC 658.4/012--dc23/eng/20230427
LC record available at https://lccn.loc.gov/2023015741
LC ebook record available at https://lccn.loc.gov/2023015742

ISBN: 978-1-032-49683-2 (hbk)
ISBN: 978-1-032-49652-8 (pbk)
ISBN: 978-1-003-39497-6 (ebk)

DOI: 10.4324/9781003394976

Typeset in Optima
by SPi Technologies India Pvt Ltd (Straive)

To my wife, Margaret, who has supported me throughout my career in ways too numerous to mention.

Contents

Acknowledgements

I would first like to acknowledge the assistance of three groups of clients over more than two decades.

The first of these are my consulting clients. These come from all sectors – business, government and not-for-profit. In the process of working closely with each, I start by understanding their industries from published data. Then, via a series of interviews with the client's staff, I gain a deeper appreciation of what the client does and the issues it faces. Then it's on to working with the board, CEO and his or her management team, assisting them to design their organization's strategy and strategic plan.

The structure of this is that of a partnership. I provide the method, while the client provides the industry and organization knowledge. A result of all this is that, as I facilitate the process, I learn a lot. I learn, for example, what works in my method and what doesn't. I learn how to better frame and write the generated objectives, develop strategies and design measures. I learn, post all of this, how the strategic plan is being implemented and how it works for them. I learn a lot, so thank you to each and every client for providing me with the opportunity.

The second group of clients I'd like to acknowledge are those who attend my public seminars. I limit the number of attendees to 25 in a room at a time so I get to hear their experiences closely. While I don't achieve the detailed, intimate contact I do with my consulting clients, I nonetheless obtain feedback about the steps I take them through. This has been immensely valuable over the 25 years I've conducted my strategic planning seminars.

The third group of clients sits between the first two and deserves to be acknowledged. They are those clients who don't wish to attend my public seminar on strategic planning but instead would like to have it run in-house for a group of managers. I end up working with individuals from one industry and organization, unlike the situation with my public seminar, but not in as much depth as with my consulting clients. I have also learnt much from these groups.

At the top of the list of individuals I'd like to name is my business partner, fellow company director and wife, Margaret Kenny. Highly qualified, holding a Bachelor of Business and Master of Commerce, she is co-author of the Strategic Factor System and has worked with me over many years to develop it. She brings to our company extensive experience in business and technology as an analyst, manager and lecturer. We work together, travel overseas to conferences together and discuss our business regularly. Margaret's support and encouragement have enabled me to press on not only with this book but with all my endeavors.

Catherine Hammond and Monique Choy have assisted with editing this book. I say "assisted," but as any writer knows, a good editor does much more than this. A good editor is a quality controller, gatekeeper and teacher. I've learnt much from Catherine and Monique about writing and expressing myself.

About the Author

Dr. Graham Kenny, CEO of Strategic Factors, is an internationally recognized expert in strategy and performance measurement. He is Australia's only regular author in the *Harvard Business Review*.

Graham is passionate about helping managers, executives and boards lead successful business, government and not-for-profit organizations.

He does this in three ways:

- Masterclasses – over 25 years as a course presenter and keynote speaker.
- Consulting – working with leaders to develop business strategy and performance scorecards.
- Publishing – through books, articles, course materials and manuals.

Graham draws on his career spanning academia, business management and leadership consulting to bring cutting-edge theory, innovation, and practical experience to his work.

He has written five books and is a panelist advisor and strategy writer for the *Harvard Business Review*.

His articles have also appeared in refereed academic journals and publications aimed at practicing managers, such as *Company Director*, *Leadership Excellence*, *Management*, *Marketing*, *Commodities & Trade to Asia*, *HR Monthly* and *Charter*.

Graham's executive experience has been considerable: as a turnaround specialist, CEO, Plant Manager, Market Development Manager, Design Engineer and Construction Supervisor.

He is a Foundation Fellow of the Australian Institute of Company Directors, a Fellow of the Institute of Managers and Leaders and a Member of the US Strategic Management Society.

Graham has been a Professor of Management at universities in the US and Canada. He holds a PhD and master's degree in management and a first degree in engineering.

Introduction

Management teams and boardrooms are in a strategy mess, confused by what strategy really is and how to design and implement it. Despite all the books, courses and articles about the topic, the meaning of strategy escapes most managers and directors. The result is corporate underperformance.

This book understands this pain and addresses it. What's more, it does so in an engaging way involving, in part, first-hand accounts and stories. It will help improve an organization's performance in significant ways, showing how to design and implement business strategy much more effectively.

Using a simple and effective framework, *Strategy Discovery* brings together the insights I've gathered over an academic career of 13 years and a management and consulting career of more than 30. This framework provides you with a methodical approach to the subject of strategy.

I expect that *Strategy Discovery* will have a wide appeal to managers and directors in organizations across all sectors – private, public and not-for-profit – because I interact with them constantly as a consultant, speaker and presenter. I also hope that it will be valued by academics, as it addresses practical pitfalls in existing strategy frameworks, it's built on a sound theoretical base and it is well referenced.

Many strategy books aimed at the professional market adopt a didactic tone. Practicing managers don't like this, and the books don't sell. Some are full of relational diagrams and dry case studies of remote organizations – another turn-off. Others are light, betraying a superficial knowledge of the topic and the literature.

My challenge was to produce a book that had substance, was practical rather than academic, but was still grounded in the literature. It's taken several re-writes to get to the finished product: a book with the following characteristics:

- Personal (it speaks to me)
- Useful (I can apply this)

DOI: 10.4324/9781003394976-1

- Actionable (I know what I need to do)
- Sound (I can see its roots in academic research and theory)

Each chapter starts with a story (personal), provides cases and examples (useful), ends with a call to implement suggested actions (actionable) and has endnotes (sound).

The opening anecdote/story is not a case study of some remote organization, but rather an account of a real-life incident. The result is, I hope: "I'm in." Each chapter then builds on this in various ways: cases, client examples, exhibits and suggestions that together provide a rich texture for the underlying framework. Chapter endings are action points, and all the content is grounded in the literature via references.

My goal in writing this book was, to use a cliché, to make a difference. By supplying an effective framework with methods to implement it, I want to assist managers and company directors improve their organizations' performance significantly.

Chapter 1

Strategic Factors

Discover the Ingredients of Success

About 20 years ago I was appointed General Manager of White River Timber, a company that made trusses and frames for houses. White River had been struggling, and my role as CEO was to turn the business around.

One fateful morning, after I'd been in the job for about three months, I found myself staring out through the large plate-glass window that formed one wall of my office, watching the trucks and forklifts below. The forklifts were dashing backwards and forwards at a frenzied pace, loading the semi-trailers. First, the timber frames went on, then the trusses, and then on top went all the other items required to construct a house. I thought, "What am I doing here? What do I know about this industry? What would I know about achieving success if I were a timber industry veteran?" It was my moment of truth.

Then came the crunch question – my *real* moment of truth. I asked myself, "What do we need to do to lift the company's performance?" I challenged myself to list, on the fingers of one hand, the ingredients of success in the industry. If I couldn't, I decided, I really shouldn't be the company's CEO.

Can I, on the fingers of one hand, tell someone the ingredients of success in this industry?

In the weeks and months that followed this startling realization, I made several significant changes in consultation with the senior management team. There were four of us on the team: the Financial Controller, the Sales Manager, the Manufacturing Manager and me. These changes included reducing staff numbers, lowering stock levels, discontinuing unprofitable product lines, closing the not-cost-effective milling operation and so on. As a team, I observed, we were busy doing things and making changes, all of which made sense to us, *as managers*. But as time progressed, I questioned how well we knew *precisely* what our customers, suppliers and employees

DOI: 10.4324/9781003394976-2

wanted. I also queried what it would take for us to meet those needs in a way that would beat our competitors. I felt that it was essential to be able to state, in a few words, the ingredients of success. And I wasn't sure I could.

Because it was a turnaround job, our management team focused primarily on cost-cutting and cost containment to save the company money. This was fine, I felt, for short-term survival, but of no *direct* benefit to the customer. Nor was it a long-term corporate solution. In fact, cutting costs could *impair* our competitive advantage by narrowing our product range and diminishing our customer service.

My reflection drew me into thinking in a way I'd now label "strategic." Until that point, as I've said, most of my focus had been on saving the company from ruin, which primarily led to "operational" thinking. Time to put some work into discovering the few fundamental ingredients of success in this industry, I thought. I needed to discover the short list of items that could see a business like ours achieve real *competitive advantage*.

Eventually, I did come up with a set of items that roughly fit on the fingers of one hand, and, as a team, we continued to make improvements. But I really wasn't happy with my list. It seemed to be a hotchpotch of items, some internal to the business, such as cost containment, and some external, like customer service. I knew I was following a common practice, but it seemed flawed.

A little over a year later, after all the tumultuous changes, we turned in the first profit that the company had achieved in a very long time. However, the holding company had other plans for its investment and sold the business. I moved on; I was happy with the results we'd achieved but not convinced by the framework I'd used.

You want to know the ingredients of success. We all do. Whether your passion is golf, tennis or cooking, you seek to uncover those basic principles which, when applied, will drive you in the right direction to succeed. And so it is with strategy. What are the few things you have to get right if your organization or business unit is to succeed?

Whether your passion is golf, tennis or cooking, you seek to uncover those basic principles which, when applied, will drive you in the right direction to succeed.

Two Kinds of Critical Success Factors

My career, post-White River Timber, took a fresh turn. Although I contemplated taking on other company turnarounds, frankly, I needed a rest. Turnarounds are tough, and I certainly didn't want to tackle another one right away. So, about a year later, after I completed a building development of my own, I began consulting for clients and conducting my first public seminars in strategic planning. In effect, I'd returned to my academic roots, but this time I was dealing with practical problems front-on and looking at the theory through a practice lens.

I started by employing the term "critical success factors" for those few things an organization has to get right to succeed.[1] This concept had been around for some time and is still in common use today. You may use it yourself in your own organization.

But the problem with the concept is that it covers a wide range of items. The "critical success factor" label is used for things as different as "market share," "capacity and productivity," "caliber of staff," "raw material costs," "engineering capability," "operating costs," "customer satisfaction" and "innovation." In short identifying "critical success factors" produces a real jumble of items.[2]

To deal with this mess, I began separating critical success factors into two categories: *competitive* and *process*. *Competitive* covered items such as customer service and product quality – external factors. Meanwhile, *process* covered activities such as selling, engineering, advertising and so on – internal factors. Note, by the way, how many activity and *process* words end in "ing." However, these labels proved quite awkward and confusing to clients. So, I had to re-think and re-design.

As I chewed on this, it became clear to me that *process* factors were second-order items as far as designing strategy was concerned, not the primary focus. *Process* factors were the operational means to achieving the *competitive* factors such as lower prices or a broader product range.

Strategy design was about taking positions on *competitive* critical success factors such as price and product range, and then using *process* factors, such as advertising, engineering and design, to implement the strategy.

Strategy aimed to achieve competitive advantage and was clearly and firmly anchored in *competitive* critical success factors. As the two labels were almost the same, I thought: could we ditch the tags altogether and simply call "competitive critical success factors" *strategic factors*?[3] I figured that the *process* critical success factors didn't need a label at all since they would re-emerge later in implementing strategy. *But*, and this is significant, their importance is governed by their link, as enablers, to positions on strategic factors.

Selecting Strategic Factors

Selecting the strategic factors for your organization is essential to your organization's success. The critical point is that strategic factors are particular to each of your organization's *stakeholders*. (We discuss stakeholders fully in the next chapter.) In the case of the stakeholder group of *customers*, for instance, I ask management teams: "What are the key things you need to get right for your customers in order to succeed?" In other words, "What are the strategic factors for your customers?" They're fundamentally the same question.

The critical point is that strategic factors are particular to each of your organization's *stakeholders*.

The answers come hesitantly at first. *Have I got this right?* the managers wonder. Then, having tested the water, they plunge in and in no time, we have the *first draft* of each key stakeholder's strategic factors.

Of course, I draw to their attention that these lists are *their* best guesses, not their key stakeholders' responses. The managers agree and take a note to verify the lists via interviews with key stakeholders later. This is critical because strategy focused on stakeholders must be developed from the stakeholders' point of view. In other words, it must be designed from the outside-in, not from the inside-out.

The process managers and directors use to verify this is interesting. From some, the response is: "My goodness, why aren't we doing this already?" They recognize the need immediately. You can see it in their eyes, on their faces. Others murmur: "Do we really need to do this?" But this disbelief turns to conviction when they realize what they've been doing for years: taking what is best for their key stakeholders for granted and, as a result, moving their business to a failure-prone position. (See Exhibit 1.1 for how managers can get it wrong.)

Stakeholder Strategic Factors

Over the years, I've assembled a large database of strategic factors – a list for each key stakeholder of *every* organization I've worked with. To assist you in your strategic-factor investigations, here are a few samples covering a range of key stakeholders across various industries.

Customers

When we think of customers, our minds naturally drift to retailing. But let's look at something different: this sample involves a government-owned port corporation we'll call Quickdoc. The company has two roles: to act as the overall authority for the port and its operations and to act as a freight handler in the port itself. The amount of work Quickdoc obtains depends on

---

Exhibit 1.1   "Information" Not a Strategic Factor

Strategic factors are the *decision criteria* a stakeholder group employs to choose one organization or business unit over another. Thus, product range, store location and price are among the criteria customers use to choose one retail outlet over another. Management groups often become confused in trying to identify strategic factors.

Take this list of strategic factors developed by a management team for the customers (current and potential residents) of a large retirement village:

- Information
- Quality of services
- Living conditions
- Range of services
- Location
- Price
- Image

Information is not a decision *criterion*, but it is an all-important *function* of the organization. Other similar terms, such as "quality of communication," may be a criterion. Of course, it goes without saying that if I, as a potential resident of the retirement village, don't know your prices, living conditions, range of services – or even the village's very existence – I won't wish to buy into it. But "information" doesn't qualify as a decision *criterion* or a strategic factor.

---

two choices by ship operators – first, they must choose Quickdoc's port over other ports in the area; second, they must choose Quickdoc to handle their freight rather than other handlers.

The central question for Quickdoc is: how do we get more business? As far as ship operators are concerned, two sets of strategic factors are involved. The first set concerns the choice of port:

- Port capability (suitability for the ship's size and freight)
- Freight availability (to pick up on the return leg)
- Congestion (speed of unloading and turnaround time in the port)
- Location ("steaming time" or time between destinations)
- Price (port charges for docking and remaining moored)

The second set concerns the choice of freight handler within the port. Here the factors are:

- Turnaround (links to rail transport, strike-free workforce, good safety record)
- Access (all-tide access)
- Charge simplicity (a one-stop shop for total logistics charges)
- Freight-handling capability (cranes and other facilities)
- Price (charges to unload and load freight)

The team at Quickdoc, composed of senior management and board members, focused on *both* sets of strategic factors and developed a strategy that would raise the corporation's performance on those factors – firstly as a port and secondly as a freight handler.

Employees

Very often, when leadership teams sit down to develop strategy, they are very focused on customers, particularly designing products that will appeal to customers. But employees are a key stakeholder group that can make or break an organization. If you can't attract and keep star performers, there's little chance that you'll be able to execute your strategic plan.

The second sample list of strategic factors concerns *employees* in a different industry: building construction.

A company we'll call Complex builds schools, office blocks, shopping centers and public facilities such as libraries and swimming pools – a broad scope of construction projects. It also refurbishes hotels, shops and restaurants. The company operates through a wide range of contractors. Complex wins the head contracts and then subcontracts most of the detailed work on each project. The management team identified the following list of strategic factors for its employees:

- Rewards (recognition, pay, bonuses and promotion opportunities)
- Development (skills training and professional development)
- Workplace environment (comfortable and safe)
- Organizational culture (ethics, working relationships, communication)
- Job security
- Job requirements (flexibility, job demands and empowerment)

The margin on the company's projects is a mere two per cent. So, in its strategic plan, management developed a strategy to attract and retain the very best staff. It recognized that achieving this edge had an additional effect on contractors and clients: both would benefit if Complex could attract and retain highly competent staff. Ultimately, there would be a significant impact on shareholders as well, showing up as above-average returns on shareholder funds.

As you would expect, I've found that strategic factors vary for the same type of key stakeholder in different industries. Safety and health concerns were paramount for the employees of a manufacturer of lead batteries where working conditions were highly toxic.

As you would expect, I've found that strategic factors vary for the same type of key stakeholder in different industries.

Suppliers

For many businesses suppliers are another key category of stakeholders. As many companies learned during the COVID pandemic, without solid relationships with suppliers, your whole business can collapse.

Consider now the case of suppliers to a mining equipment company we'll call Equip. It manufactures replacement parts for major earthmoving and drilling equipment. Equip's suppliers provide materials and component parts to produce these replacements. The management team identified the following strategic factors for their suppliers:

* Profitability (the margin between make and sell)
* Lead time (to prepare the order – the longer, the better)
* Specifications (clear details of what is required)
* Payment (promptly and with minimal red tape)
* Business-growth opportunities (through a long-term relationship)

Equip's management team recognized the importance of doing well on these factors if its relationships with its suppliers were to be effective and not hinder its relationship with its customers. To cite one example, Equip set out to improve its performance on lead time by establishing an information system that ensured suppliers had advance notice of Equip's requirements. This led to better performance by Equip itself in meeting *its* customers' deadlines.

Key Result Area vs. Strategic Factor

A widespread practice in developing so-called "strategies" goes like this: During the strategic planning session, the suggestion will be made to identify the organization's "critical success factors," "key result areas (KRAs)," or some other general-purpose label for the ingredients of success.[4] Someone will walk over to a flipchart or whiteboard and write a heading, and everyone will pile in to come up with a short list of items.

Let's take a look at several sets of such results derived from this approach. One concerns the World Customs Organization. Listed online as KRAs are:

- International cooperation and information sharing
- Harmonization and simplification of customs systems and procedures
- Compliance and enforcement
- Trade facilitation
- Supply chain security and facilitation
- Capacity building
- Promotion and marketing
- Research and analysis
- Good governance and use of resources

Here are the KRAs for the Aircraft Certification Business Plan:

- Implementation of safety management systems
- Enhancing industry relationships
- Enhancing the certification program
- Ensuring adequate regulatory materials and policies
- Enhancing management processes and practices
- Implementation of the accountability framework and safety management systems for aeronautical product certification

The Plastics Sector Council also lists seven key result areas to guide its strategies and activities:

- Career awareness/promotion
- Labor market research
- Training
- Job competencies
- Career development/continuing education
- Accreditation
- Qualification/recognition

Items such as these, generated in the manner I've described, which then become the focus of developing "strategy," don't always carry the classic labels "KRA" or "critical success factor." There are numerous synonyms such as "priorities," "domains," "key success factors," "priority areas" and even "key objectives." But the result is always the same: a set of business-as usual items developed by a group of managers sitting in a room. It's all too comfortable to be challenging – or useful.

But the result is always the same: a set of business-as-usual items developed by a group of managers sitting in a room. It's all too comfortable to be challenging – or useful.

Note how bland these items are compared to the varied sets of strategic factors described earlier. I've identified four fundamental differences between the critical-success-factors/KRA approach and the strategic-factors approach: see Exhibit 1.2. Remember these when next you're tempted to look inside-out (critical success factors/KRAs) rather than outside-in (strategic factors).

Exhibit 1.2   Different Features

Feature	Critical Success Factors/ Key Result Areas	Strategic Factors
Number of Sets of Factors	One per organization or business unit	One per stakeholder group, e.g., customers, employees, suppliers
Who Identifies Them	The management team	The management team, *but only as a first draft*
Who Validates and Defines Them	The management team	Stakeholders
Workshop Atmosphere	Competitive and combative	Constructive and inquiring

---

The first major difference is the number of sets, and this is fundamental to your strategic planning and the development of strategies. With critical success factors and KRAs, there is *one set per organization or business unit*. With strategic factors, there is *one set per stakeholder* – one for your customers, one for your employees, one for your suppliers and so on. For example, instead of the KRA called "people management," which is very broad, a strategic-factor approach would substitute this with the *key stakeholder* called employees and *then* identify the specific strategic factors for this group. These include rewards, work location, coworker relationships, promotional opportunities and job demands. A strategy would be developed around these items to achieve a competitive advantage in attracting and retaining effective staff.

With strategic factors, there is *one set per stakeholder* – one for your customers, one for your employees, one for your suppliers and so on.

Take the fast-food chains KFC and Burger King. The strategic factors for their *customers* are product range, product quality, company image, customer service, store location, store presentation, hours of operation, and price. Again, a strategy to achieve competitive advantage would be developed around these factors. A different set of factors exists for each of these chains' other stakeholders such as *employees*, *shareholders* and *suppliers*.

The second and third points of difference are who identifies and who validates the factors/areas. This is a matter of great practical significance for you. Critical success factors and KRAs are determined *by the management team* of an organization or business unit. Typically, as I have noted, a manager will walk over to a whiteboard or flipchart and write "critical success factors" or "key result areas" on top of it. Then the management team strives to come up with items they think should make the shortlist.

As is usually the case in these situations, rank plays an important part. The more senior the manager, the more he or she is likely to get his or her item accepted. The CEO has huge clout. Different personalities also play a part. The persuasive and boisterous outbid the shy.[5] A list is developed at the end of a process like this, but you should ask: Is the list valid? The fact that it can only be "validated" by your management should cause flashing red lights to go off in your head.

With strategic factors, the situation is completely different. While the factors may be developed *initially* by your management team, the team agrees that this is only a starting point. Each list, one per key stakeholder, *must* be subsequently *validated by researching the requirements of each key stakeholder*. This is essential if you are to develop effective strategy later.

Each list, one per key stakeholder, *must* be subsequently *validated by researching the requirements of each key stakeholder*.

An additional practical impact I've observed concerns the atmosphere in these "critical success factor/KRA" vs. "strategic factor" sessions. It is very different. In the "critical success factor/KRA" sessions, the climate is competitive, combative and sometimes downright hostile. In the "strategic factor" sessions, the atmosphere is far more constructive and inquiring as the aim is to see the organization or business unit through the eyes of stakeholders. As a result, the heat is off individual management team members to compete for a point. The emphasis shifts from an inside-out view of what the organization does, the "critical-success-factor/KRA" approach, to an outside-in view of what stakeholders want, the "strategic-factor" approach.

Your Fresh Approach

When next you think about the ingredients of success for your organization or business unit, when next you stare out your metaphorical plate-glass window searching for answers, take the following few fundamental steps.

Change Your Thinking. Think outside-in. You know how easy it is to get drawn in by operational detail, to become swamped by the processes and procedures of your organization. But you have recognized the need to step out of your organization and look at it outside-in. It's a discipline that will pay dividends.

Identify Key Stakeholders. Identify the *key* stakeholders of your organization or business unit and then look at what you do through their eyes. Here lie your stakeholder's strategic factors and your organization's ingredients of success. Your stakeholders will be groups such as customers, suppliers, employees and owners.

Focus on Strategic Factors. Ask: What makes them buy from/supply to/ work for/invest in your organization or business unit? This is outside-in thinking. You'll come up with items like product quality for customers, order lead time for suppliers, promotional prospects for employees and capital growth for owners. These strategic factors are the key ingredients of your organization's success.[6]

Notes

1 According to John Rockart, the concept of "success factors" was first discussed in management literature in 1961 by Ronald Daniel. As Daniel put it in his seminal contribution: "In most industries there are usually three to six factors that determine success; these key jobs must be done exceedingly well for a company to be successful." Rockart went on to explain critical success factors this way: "Critical success factors thus are, for any business, the limited number of areas in which results, if they are satisfactory, will ensure successful competitive performance for the organization. They are the few key areas where things must go right for the business to flourish. If results in these areas are not adequate, the organization's efforts for the period will be less than desired. As a result, the critical success factors are areas of activity that should receive constant and careful attention from management. The current status of performance in each area should be continually measured, and that information should be made available." Daniel's and Rockart's concerns were with focusing management information systems. See Daniel, D.R. 1961. Management information crisis. *Harvard Business Review*, September–October: 111–121; and Rockart, J. 1979. Chief executives define their own data needs. *Harvard Business Review*, March–April: 81–93.

2　It appears that the US academics Charles Hofer and Dan Schendel were primarily responsible for applying the critical success factors concept to *business strategy*. See Hofer, C.W. & Schendel, D. 1978. *Strategy formulation: Analytical concepts*. St Paul: West Publishing. Kenichi Ohmae uses the terms "key factors for success" but this refers to a *single* factor within an industry that drives the success of the leading competitors, e.g., economies of scale in shipbuilding and steelmaking (p. 38). See Ohmae, K., 1983. *The mind of the strategist: Business planning for competitive advantage*. New York: Penguin. Among more modern *textbook* examples of Ohmae's use of the term, see Hubbard, G., Rice, J. & Beamish, P. 2008. *Strategic management: Thinking, analysis, action*. Frenchs Forest: Pearson Education.

3　The "strategic factors" label was finally adopted following a conversation I had with my wife, Margaret, in Auckland, New Zealand, on the weekend of May 15–16, 1999, after the strategic planning seminar that I had conducted. While "critical success factors" appeared in the brochures for my seminars in October 1999 – the brochures are prepared some months in advance of the seminar date – the term had disappeared completely and been replaced by "strategic factors" in the brochures for my March 2000 seminars. The term "critical success factors" was never to be used again.

4　I've been unable to trace the exact origin of "key result area." However, Peter Drucker provides eight "key areas" in which "objectives of performance and results have to be set." See his chapter "The Objectives of a Business" in his 1955 book *The Practice of Management*. London: Pan Books. John Rockart equates "critical success factors" with "key areas." (See the earlier quote from him in note 1.)

5　I think this is what concerned Argenti when he raised doubts in his book about employing critical success factors as a device. He writes: "In the company where I witnessed [critical success factors'] use it was virtually ignored by the senior executives, most of whom felt that little reliance could be placed on its accuracy. They did not agree with the ranking that the planning department had ascribed to the factors; some did not accept some of the factors at all, others proposed additional ones, others quarreled with the place given to the company compared to its competitors, some wanted to add or subtract competitors from the list, others disagreed with the stated scope for management action." See Argenti, J. 1989. *Practical corporate planning*. London: Routledge, p. 218.

6　Strategic factors became well and truly cemented in our system with the publication of my 2001 book entitled *Strategic factors: Develop and measure winning strategy*. Sydney: President Press (republished in 2005 as *Strategic planning and performance management*. Oxford: Elsevier Butterworth-Heinemann).

Chapter 2

Stakeholders

Unearth Latent Dependencies

I was once facilitating a strategic planning session for an organization dedicated to educating individuals with autism and providing support to their families. It operates special schools, trains parents in the care of autistic children, supplies information about autism to the public, and funds research into the causes and management of autism.

The organization's board and senior management were present at the workshop – in all, 13 people. My task was to assist this group in developing the strategic plan. We had just come to the point of identifying the organization's *key* stakeholders, and I was taking suggestions to write on the whiteboard. I had "funders" (those who provide funds to the organization, such as the government), "clients" (individuals with autism and their families) and "employees." Then, out of habit, I added "suppliers."

Someone asked, "Are they really *key*?" I had to think.

"Who are your suppliers?" I asked. "I mean, do companies supply your organization with paper, computer supplies and so on?"

"Yes, that's right," came the response from the Financial Controller.

"Just incidental items, then?" I asked.

"Yes," the group agreed.

"So," I continued, wanting to ensure we all understood, "your relationship with your suppliers is not like Toyota or McDonald's. If Toyota gets poor parts from its suppliers, this affects the quality of its cars and, in turn, customer satisfaction and sales. So, suppliers have a *fundamental* and *direct* impact on customers – and on Toyota's success. It's the same with McDonald's. If its suppliers provide poor hamburger patties or bread rolls, McDonald's customers suffer, and so does McDonald's. Are you like that with your suppliers?" I enquired.

"Not at all," said the CEO. "Being in the service sector, it's employees that have the direct, and major, impact."

"Well, in that case, it seems to me that, for you, suppliers aren't key," I offered. "In fact," I continued, with a further light going on in my head,

DOI: 10.4324/9781003394976-3

"your relationship with them is more *operational* than *strategic*. They're almost like a department *within* your organization. Have I got that right?" (This was the first time this sequence of conceptual links had gone off in my brain.)

"Yes," came the chorus. "Suppliers *aren't* key."

On the surface, it may seem easy to identify an organization's or business unit's key stakeholders. *Surely, we know that!* people probably think. But it's not as easy as it looks. When I assisted the management group of a government department responsible for infrastructure policy, they took nearly *three hours* to work it out. They had to decide who their stakeholders were, which ones were "key," whether some key stakeholders occupied two roles (e.g., "community" and "clients"), and whether some key stakeholder classifications should be separated or combined.

On the surface, it may seem easy to identify an organization's or business unit's key stakeholders.

Another time I worked with a credit union management team who had trouble deciding who its *customers* were – the borrowers or the lenders? And another client, the senior executives and academics of a university, wrestled with whether its students or industry employers were its "customers." Then there was the CEO of an electrical goods manufacturer who used the term "customer" so generically that he became confused about whether "customers" referred to retailers or end users. And the management team of a producer of payroll systems software queried whether competitors were also stakeholders.

In the previous chapter, I repeatedly referred to "stakeholders" and "key stakeholders."[1] As you now understand, strategic factors are the criteria that stakeholders apply to your organization's or business unit's performance. It goes without saying that you better know them well if you have any intentions of succeeding. But who exactly are stakeholders? And how would you identify those that are key?

Why Stakeholders?

Whole Foods Market dominates natural foods retailing in the US and has become an iconic brand. Its co-founder and co-CEO, John Mackey, spoke about its great success over 30 years in a *Harvard Business Review* interview. Mackey described his "stakeholder model" and "stakeholder philosophy":

> You have to recognize the stakeholder model: Customers, employees, investors, suppliers, larger communities, and the environment are all

interdependent. You operate the business in such a way that it's not a zero-sum game… Management's job at Whole Foods is to make sure that we hire good people, that they are well trained, and that they flourish in the workplace, because we found that when people are really happy in their jobs, they provide much higher degrees of service to the customers. Happy team members result in happy customers. Happy customers do more business with you. They become advocates for your enterprise, which results in happy investors. That is a win, win, win, win strategy. You can expand it to include your suppliers and the communities where you do business, which are tied into this prosperity circle. A metaphor I like is the spiral, which tends to move upward but doesn't move in a straight line.[2]

Stakeholders are organizations, groups and, in some cases, individuals on which your organization or business unit depends for success. The four stereotypes – customers, employees, suppliers and owners – are illustrated in Exhibit 2.1, which also shows that transactions occur between these groups and an organization. A business, for example, gives goods or services to customers – and receives money in return.

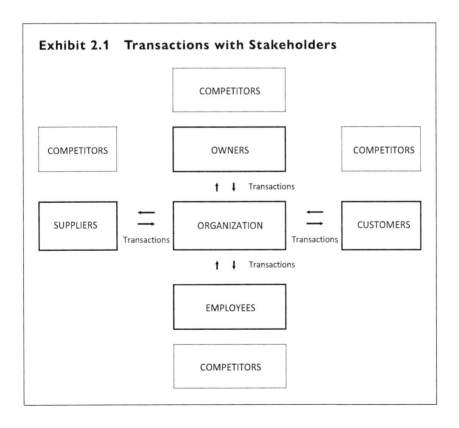

Exhibit 2.1 Transactions with Stakeholders

Stakeholders are organizations, groups and, in some cases, individuals on which your organization or business unit depends for success.

Under a stakeholder view, an organization becomes a corporate shell through which inputs, of various kinds, are converted into outputs, of various types. This shell is also a legal entity, because in company law an organization can enter contracts and be held legally liable – just as you and I can. "Shell" and "legal entity" are at least two of the ways we can conceive of an organization in a stakeholder framework.

A stakeholder framework is also consistent with social systems theory. An entity, in this case an organization or business, survives through importing and exporting *energy*. The energy comes from and goes to stakeholders. The growth and strength of an organization is determined by this importing and exporting process. The decision-makers *within* the organization are its senior managers, embodied in the CEO. Interestingly, senior managers wear two hats. They're both employees, paid by the organization, and decision-makers/arbitrators in the exchange process. They conduct the market, if you will.

You might note that competitors have *not* been listed as stakeholders. Some formulations do.[3] Competitors are in fact the *antithesis* of a stakeholder. They actually try to lure stakeholders away from an organization. As Exhibit 2.1 illustrates, competitors are numerous, for example, for an organization's customers, both current and potential. There is an even larger set of competitors for its employees, again current and potential. Another set exists for its suppliers and another for its owners – yes, because owners can invest elsewhere. In every case, competitors are doing their best to get stakeholders to abandon the organization.

Varying Importance of Stakeholders

Stakeholders can play varied roles in establishing and sustaining an enterprise. The role of owners initially is to supply funds to the company. This flows through the organizational system and is linked to employees as wages. These generate ongoing employee effort, which assists in the purchase of supplies. Customers are provided with goods and services and in turn remit their payments. This profit ultimately flows back to owners, in the form of dividends. Owners stand at the end of the queue when it comes to returns and at the head of it when it comes to capital supplied.

Are owners (shareholders) the most important stakeholder? If they are, why do we often hear CEOs saying, "Employees are our most important asset," "Customers are key" or "The consumer is king"?

The answer is that different stakeholders are more or less important for different reasons and at different times. Each supplies inputs that sustain an organization in diverse ways. In an already established organization, customers are paramount in the supply of operating revenue. Without operating revenue, a business goes bust. However, if we start with suppliers, we see that *they* are all-important in the input of goods-and-services, without which an organization seizes up. It's also plain to see that if we commence with employees, they stand tall in the supply of physical and intellectual effort, without which there can be no organization at all.

The answer is that different stakeholders are more or less important for different reasons and at different times.

While stakeholders differ in their importance on issues, overall, it still is possible, and highly necessary for resource-allocation purposes, to identify an inner sanctum of stakeholders – those I call "key."

Which Stakeholders Are "Key"?

Working out who your *key* stakeholders are *does* take time, and it *is* a little tricky – and, as Exhibit 2.2 illustrates, can become somewhat messy. But it is important as Deanna Robinson, Head of Monitoring and Vendor Development at US clothing producers and retailer, Gap Inc., told the *MIT Sloan Management Review*:

> We recognized that it would not be possible for us to have a strategic relationship with each of the stakeholders, so we highlighted those who we deemed to be the most key.

Daryl Knudsen, Gap's Director of Public Policy and Stakeholder Engagement, also explained:

> We will never be able to engage at the same level of depth with every organization that exists but by engaging with organizations who themselves have extensive networks, we have managed to receive some level of input and influence from those networks.[4]

"Are they really *key*?" is the question I often hear in sessions. To help address this, I've developed five tests for a key stakeholder, listed in Exhibit 2.3. Employ these when next you're faced with the issue.[5]

Exhibit 2.2   Managers Get Confused About Stakeholders

It's easy for managers to become confused about an organization's key stakeholders. The CEO, three directors, and four other senior managers from a fruit-packing company met to prepare the company's strategic plan and identified the following as key stakeholders:

- Shareholders
- Growers – Packing
- Growers – Marketing
- Customers
- Input Suppliers/Service Providers
- Employees
- Directors

They'd split the grower stakeholder group into those that required the packing service only, "Growers – Packing," and those that required the packing and marketing service, "Growers – Marketing," on the basis that each group's strategic factors were different. No problems there. But they'd added "Directors" as a key stakeholder. I pointed out that while the directors may be the mouthpieces of the shareholders, they are *never* stakeholders. Nor is a board.

A board and directors sit inside the organization's "circle" when it comes to stakeholders. The board is ultimately responsible for an organization's performance and delegates this responsibility to a CEO, who runs the organization.

Exhibit 2.3   Five Tests for a Key Stakeholder

Test	Required Response	Example
1. Do they have a fundamental impact on organizational performance?	☑ Yes ☐ No	A local council may be a stakeholder of an organization but, unlike customers, it does not substantially impact organizational performance. So, it is not a *key* stakeholder.

2. Can you clearly identify what you want from them?	☑ Yes ☐ No	The management team of a law firm nominated clients, employees, partners and the community as *key* stakeholders. Yet it couldn't specify what it wanted *from* the community. Its relationship with the community was therefore neither strategic nor *key*.
3. Is the relationship dynamic?	☑ Yes ☐ No	A company that ran 17 retirement villages had a dynamic relationship with its current and potential residents. It wanted more. Its relationship with a university, which involved research funding and co-badging, was static. Badging was simply a one-off action to improve the company's image – though this image was indeed a strategic factor for many stakeholders. As a result, the university did not achieve "key" stakeholder status.
4. Can you exist without them or easily replace them?	☐ Yes ☑ No	A bank may be a stakeholder because the company has a loan from it. But that loan could be easily refinanced with another bank. The bank is not a *key* stakeholder.
5. Has this stakeholder already been identified via another relationship? (double counting)	☐ Yes ☑ No	If a management team nominates both employees and unions as stakeholders, this is double counting because unions represent employees' interests. It is the employees who are the *key* stakeholders in this case.

The Main Roads Department in one of Australia's largest states is a public-sector organization that oversees the major roads and highways in that state. It covers an extremely large area and has over 1,000 employees. Contractors play a major part in its operations. By applying the five tests, I assisted its senior management team in producing the list of key stakeholders below. This list also illustrates the clumping together of groups, those in brackets, to narrow down the initial, rather long, list.

- Minister (Elected Member of Parliament responsible for state infrastructure)
- Central Agencies (Treasury, other government departments, Federal Government)
- Road Users (Car, truck and bike owners, pedestrians, public transport organizations and representative groups)
- Local Government as Partner (Local government organizations throughout the State with whom Main Roads needs to work to develop and maintain the road network)
- Affected Community (Landowners adjacent to roads, major developers, advocacy groups)
- Services Providers (Contractors, consultants, suppliers)
- Employees

Here are several other key-stakeholder lists developed with clients by employing the tests in Exhibit 2.3. In each case, the definition given was developed by the organization. The first example concerns a buying group of 265 members, each of whom owned one or more jewelry stores and who, together as shareholders, owned the buying group. Bradco's key stakeholders were:

- Customers (Individuals targeted by Bradco members who buy or could buy products and services from Bradco members)
- Suppliers (Organizations that provide products and services to Bradco members via Bradco)
- Employees (Individuals who provide their personal skills to Bradco)
- Members-as-Retailers (Jewelry business members that rely on Bradco as a buying, marketing and advisory group)
- Members-as-Shareholders (Jewelry business members in their role as the owners of Bradco)

Another list concerns the not-for-profit developer and manager of several retirement villages. The key stakeholders for Horizon were:

- Retirement Living Clients (Individuals who reside or could reside in Horizon's self-care retirement villages)
- Residential Aged-Care Clients (Individuals who reside or could reside in Horizon's aged-care facilities)
- Care-in-the-Home Clients (Individuals who receive or could receive Horizon's services in their homes)
- Staff (Individuals who provide their personal skills to Horizon for benefit)
- Health-Care Providers (Organizations and individuals who provide referrals and health support to Horizon)
- Government-as-Funder (Government agencies responsible for the provision of subsidies to Horizon)
- Volunteers (Individuals and groups who give their time to Horizon without pay)
- Donors (Individuals and organizations who give financial support to Horizon)
- Owners (The parent organization that established and governs Horizon via a board appointed by it)

The next list, with even more variety, concerns a large practice of specialist surgeons. Its key stakeholders were:

- Patients (Individuals and families who use the services of the practice)
- Medical Referrers (General practitioners, other specialists and emergency departments who refer patients to the practice)
- Legal/Third-Party Referrers (Insurers and lawyers who refer patients to the practice for examination and an independent medical opinion)
- Hospitals (Tertiary facilities that deliver surgical and medical services and where the surgeons operate)
- Employees (Persons other than surgeons who provide their skills to the practice for reward)
- Surgeons (Neurosurgeons who perform surgery within the practice)
- Shareholders (Individuals and related entities who own the practice)

With a further twist, the final list involves the operator of several cemeteries and crematoria. Condell Park's key stakeholders were:

- Families/Community (People who use or could use cemetery and crematorium services, including individuals associated with families who could recommend Condell Park, e.g., religious groups, local community groups, etc.)

- Funeral Directors (Organizations that use or could use Condell Park's facilities)
- Contractors/Suppliers (Organizations and individuals who provide services and products to Condell Park, e.g., caterers, cleaners, electricians, earthworks and maintenance contractors)
- Employees (Individuals who provide skills and personal services to Condell Park)
- Holding Company (The company that owns Condell Park and represents the ultimate shareholders)

Targeting Stakeholders

Lists of key stakeholders like those above may not convey what a very important next step in the identification process is. It is *targeting*. This is the next-level-down step.

When it comes to "customers," for example, not all customers in your industry are *your* customers. The same is true for suppliers, employees and investors. Not all should be the target of your strategies. In the case of Rolex customers, for example, not all watch customers are Rolex customers; Rolex knows that and must never forget it in its strategic planning.

As another example, take the large Australian retail department-store chain, David Jones. Its target *customer* was the 30–54-year-old, higher-income woman. But it also targeted its other stakeholders in its turnaround some years ago. Regarding *employees*: certain staff had to be let go as they didn't fit the customer-service profile required by the targeted customers, while other staff who did fit had to be hired. As for *suppliers*: only certain ones could fill the bill on product quality, image/brand and supply reliability. As to *shareholders*, only certain institutions supported DJ's new direction and believed that the department-store concept had a future in modern retailing. The corporate results since DJ's re-focus wouldn't have happened without clear targeting across its range of key stakeholders.

The Pan Pacific Hotels Group operates scores of hotels, resorts and serviced suites with over 10,000 rooms in the US, South-East Asia, China and Australia. Its CEO, Patrick Imbardelli, had this to say about "targeting" within stakeholders and strategy:

> In today's environment, it's about building the service and structure of a hotel to specifically look after one market. For example, if we look at the hotel we are building now in Singapore, it is definitely a corporate hotel. It's technology-driven and specifically pitched at 30–48-year-olds. So, we have made the decision that the hotel doesn't have to appeal to people outside this demographic. We came to that conclusion because

customers are now saying that if they come and stay in a particular city and it's for business, there is a high likelihood they will stay in a different hotel than if they were visiting for leisure. Most hotel brands try to be everything to everyone, which can still succeed, but at a huge cost. They are the most vulnerable.[6]

Finally, it's important to appreciate that the needs and wants of your key stakeholders keep changing, as does what your organization can offer them. Engaging in this ebb and flow and coming to certain positions, temporary though they may be, is the key role of your senior management and a vital ingredient in producing successful strategy for your organization.

You may never have approached strategy development and your strategic plan's structuring via a stakeholder framework.

Your Stakeholder Focus

You may never have approached strategy development and your strategic plan's structuring via a stakeholder framework. If not, it's time to change. On the other hand, you may have attempted to do so and have struggled to follow through completely. In either case, here are a few steps to follow:

Re-Think. Start thinking "stakeholders." This requires viewing your organization in the abstract. That is, you must take a systems view of its operation, divorcing yourself from personal involvement. Place yourself in a helicopter above all the to-ing and fro-ing that takes place *in* your organization. From that viewpoint, looking down, note the transactions, exchanges and interactions that take place, or could take place, between your organization or business unit and its stakeholders.

Focus on "Key." Note how some of your organization's stakeholders are more important to its survival and growth than others. Apply the tests for "key" from Exhibit 2.3 to narrow the field. One CEO described the benefits of this focus: "As a CEO, I was always dealing with different people around the board table driving the virtues of a particular stakeholder. Now the organization and the board know who our most important stakeholders are, and where we should be directing our attention, energy and resources."[7]

Target within Key. Make sure that in the final analysis, you address not just "key" but "target." Targeting specific groups within your stakeholder categories is essential if your organization or business unit intends to make its mark, rise above the pack, write clear and focused strategy and achieve significant competitive advantage.

Notes

1 Moving to "stakeholders" may take time. In 1983, when I was Visiting Associate Professor in the School of Business at the University of Alberta, I received an advance copy of a book that has since become highly significant. At the time I ignored it. (Freeman, R.E. 1984. *Strategic management: A stakeholder approach.* Marshfield: Pitman Publishing.) I ignored it because the strategy textbooks at that time did not acknowledge "stakeholders." They certainly weren't built on a stakeholder framework and, to my knowledge, none *in print* today are either. Strategic management textbooks then and now are an eclectic collection of different frameworks. I first commenced consulting and conducting my public seminars on strategic planning towards the end of 1989. The framework that I adopted then was still devoid of "stakeholders." Although my approach went through a number of transformations, it remained basically the same until my seminars of July 1996. The seminar brochure from that time lists the program and in it is a topic, "Developing a Strategy." Under this heading is a sub-point, "Relating strategy to stakeholders." Stakeholders had made the agenda a full 13 years after I received Freeman's book! Later that year, in the brochures for the November 1996 seminars, stakeholders warranted a subtitle of their own! It was "Recognizing Key Stakeholders." In preparing this chapter I revisited several books and articles on organization–environment relations that I found foundational to my own thinking over the last 30 years. They've also influenced, some in quite indirect ways, the long-term development of the ideas in this book. Most I hadn't looked at in many years. What was noticeable was the lack of reference to "stakeholder," yet it would have been a useful, even fundamental, concept in most cases. Here is just a sample: Thompson, J.D. 1967. *Organizations in action.* New York: McGraw Hill; Lawrence, P.R. & Lorsch, J.W. 1967. *Organization and environment.* Boston: Harvard University Press; Pfeffer, J. & Salancik, G.R. 1978. *The external control of organizations: A resource dependence perspective.* New York: Harper & Row; Aldrich, H.E. 1979. *Organizations and environments.* Englewood Cliffs: Prentice-Hall; Scott, W.R. 1981. *Organizations: Rational, natural and open systems.* Englewood Cliffs: Prentice-Hall.

2 Interview: What is it that only I can do? *Harvard Business Review,* 2011, January–February: 119–123.

3 Early authors such as Freeman, *Strategic management: A stakeholder approach,* and Mitroff, I.I., 1983, *Stakeholders of the organizational mind.* San Francisco: Jossey-Bass, take a broader view of stakeholders and include competitors. Some more current authors continue to take this view. See, for example, Hart, S.L. & Sharma, S. 2004. Engaging fringe stakeholders for competitive imagination. *Academy of Management Executive,* 18(1): 7–18. Others have noted this as an error – see Post, J.E., Preston, L.E. & Sachs, S. 2002. *Redefining the corporation: Stakeholder management and organizational wealth.* Stanford: Stanford Business Books.

4 Smith, N.C., Ansett, S. & Erez, L. 2011. How Gap Inc. engaged with its stakeholders. *MIT Sloan Management Review,* Summer: 69–76, p. 72.

5 Further discussion on what makes stakeholders important can be found in Mitchell, R.K., Agle, B.R. & Wood, D.J. 1997. Toward a theory of stakeholder identification and salience: Defining the principle of who and what really counts. *Academy of Management Review,* 22(4): 853–886; Cummings, J.L. &

Doh, J.P. 2000. Identifying who matters: Mapping key players in multiple environments. *California Management Review*, 42(2): 83–104.

6 Conroy, S. 2011. The sustainable CEO. *Management Today*, August: 8–11, p. 10.

7 Quote by Elaine Henry, then the CEO of the Smith Family, a large not-for-profit organization in Australia that caters for the needs of disadvantaged children and their families. From Moodie A. 2009. When the benefit is mutual. *Australian School of Business Magazine*, 10: 30–31, p. 31.

Chapter 3

Business Models

Reveal Hidden Business Design

I was once facilitating a strategic planning session for a group of managers in charge of a canned fruit and vegetable co-operative. The company also had a frozen-food plant that packaged corn cobs, peas, beans and other vegetables. I'll call the business Farmers' Best. It's grower owned.

On this day, I had around 18 people in the room, from the CEO down. I clearly remember a point in our discussion when "customers" came up. Individuals chipped in with what they thought "customers" wanted. I got very confused.

"Hold it," I said, turning to the Operations Manager. "Who's the customer?"

"The retailers," he replied. This was one group that we had already identified as a key stakeholder.

I then turned to the Marketing Manager and asked the same question. "The people who eat our products," she declared.

"So," I blurted, "you're using the same label to describe two different stakeholders – the retailers and the end users! Is that right?"

"Yes," they admitted. The confusion this caused was obvious, and we settled on the terms "Customers" for retailers and "Consumers" for end users.

What I also noticed during our detailed discussions was that only a few of those 18 people really understood the organization's *business model* – me included.[1] In the group were individuals who had held their specialist roles for years in sales, manufacturing, IT, HR and so on. Their knowledge of Farmers' Best was confined to their specialty area. On a day-to-day basis, they only addressed issues in their narrow domains. Yet here we were, developing strategies that concerned the business *as a whole*. As a group, we needed to understand how the business operated and succeeded – its business model. So, on the whiteboard, I started to sketch out how the co-operative made a profit from go to whoa, from grower to consumer.

DOI: 10.4324/9781003394976-4

What I also noticed during our detailed discussions was that only a few of those 18 people really understood the organization's *business model* – me included.

And that's what a business model is: the way a business in the private sector generates revenue and makes a profit.[2] (See Exhibit 3.1 for an illustration from the airline industry.) In the not-for-profit sector, it's how an organization obtains funds and balances its books. In the public sector, it's how a government organization works within budget to deliver services effectively and efficiently.[3]

Exhibit 3.1   Ryanair Changes Its Business Model

These days we're all familiar with budget airlines. Ireland's Ryanair was one of the pioneers. In the early 1990s, it switched from the industry's traditional business model to one that was low-priced. It did away with all frills, flew out of secondary airports, catered only to one class of passenger, charged for all extra services, didn't serve meals, made only short-distance flights and employed a standard fleet of Boeing 737s. Through other cost-saving measures, including cutting labor costs via a non-unionized workforce and running a lean head office, Ryanair achieved an acceptable level of service at a low price that suited its target, budget and customer, producing a high volume of passengers. It changed not only its own business model but that of an industry.

Simple and Complex Business Models

Sunshine Living is a not-for-profit organization owned by another not-for-profit organization. The parent organization exerts its influence via the board it appoints. Sunshine Living operates 17 retirement villages and aged-care facilities. My task was to assist the board, CEO and senior management team in developing a strategic plan for the next five years.

Sunshine Living has been very successful, especially in recent years, having grown rapidly, mainly through acquisition. It purchased the other properties mostly from for-profit businesses struggling to turn a profit. Sunshine Living's business model gave the organization an operational advantage because it could function more easily within government funding constraints. It didn't need to make a profit. As a result, it could balance its books and deliver better care within a fixed budget than a private operator – in theory, at least.

But that was only one aspect of Sunshine Living's business model, as I discovered. How did I get to the point of needing to document its business model at all?

The first issue was the complexity of the model. With some businesses, it's easy to see how things work. In retailing, a business buys and sells, and having quickly come to grips with this business model, you can move on to designing a strategy that will lead to competitive advantage. In other situations, the funding streams and charge arrangements are intricate, and the industry is changing. This was the case with Sunshine Living.

The second issue was that our executive group of 12, with me as the facilitator, wasn't progressing. We had identified Sunshine Living's key stakeholders, organization objectives and strategic factors, but from that point in our strategic planning, the sessions lacked what I can only describe as "punch." It was quickly becoming business-as-usual.[4]

I felt the solution was to pull these deliberations together to give them focus: to summarize and articulate Sunshine Living's business model for the group, and for me. So, I called the CEO to go through it with him. Notice how stakeholders weave their way through the model and the narrative.[5]

Owners

We figured out that Sunshine Living's model begins with *owners*, the parent organization. It had given the CEO the green light to grow, provided that any growth was sustainable, not making a loss. There were no specific five-year targets, but it was clear that this growth would come mainly from acquisition. Over the past few years, for-profit operators had brought opportunities to Sunshine Living for purchase. The decision was made for this process to continue into the future.

Clients

The second driver of growth concerned growth *within* the existing 17 establishments. For example, in one case, this meant the expansion of the village to provide more rooms for individuals requiring aged care.

The retirement/aged-care industry comprises three levels.

- **First level**. This involves retirement-living clients who reside in self-contained apartments and townhouses and look after themselves.

However, they live on an estate that offers support from the central office if needed. The residents don't own the property they live in but instead lease it, having exclusive use of it for the duration of their occupancy. They pay a "bond," which is returned, less a calculated amount, on a resident's departure. They also pay a monthly levy for the property's use, maintenance, lawn mowing, gardening, recreational facilities, 24-hour emergency call service and so on. Sunshine Living gets to keep the interest on all bond monies, and it expands this line of business by building more dwellings.

- **Second level**. Retirement-living clients may progress to the second level of care by becoming aged-care clients. This group comprises single individuals who live in a small apartment, complete with a bathroom, but come together for meals provided by the establishment in one communal space. Each room lacks cooking facilities but has emergency cords and buttons should an individual require assistance. These residents also pay a bond, and Sunshine Living balances its books with them by a combination of interest on bonds and a daily-care fee. The latter is automatically subsidized by the Australian Government, with the remaining element paid for either by the Government or the individual, depending on the individual's means. Growth in this business area comes about through building more rooms – "beds" in industry parlance.
- **Third level**. This occurs in individuals' homes: *care-in-the-home clients*. The Australian Government has determined that it's more cost-effective to keep aging individuals in their own homes and bring the services to them. It's called "Aging in Place." This part of the business model is fee-for-service. As this is a relatively new initiative, Sunshine Living is not well represented here and is currently not well structured to provide it.

Staff

Staff also enter the business model. Because of the industry and because it's so heavily government-funded, Sunshine Living is greatly restricted in what it can pay its staff. Charges to clients and profit margins are limited, so wages are naturally squeezed, particularly with carer employees. The result is high employee turnover in some of Sunshine Living's retirement villages that require long travel times to and from work. For example, the head office and largest establishment are located in an affluent area. Care employees do not come from this area – clients do. The employees come from the other side of the city. As a result, travel times and travel costs are high for these individuals, but wages are low. Hence the high turnover.

Overall employee productivity is also an important driver in the business model and, where possible, needs to be raised.

Government

The government greatly impacts Sunshine Living, mainly through funding for places. The latter is applied through formulas relating to a person's particular situation. Once these formulas are applied, Sunshine Living's revenue stream becomes quite stable. To maintain it, the organization needs to demonstrate compliance. This stakeholder group was labeled *governments* to cover all three levels of government, federal, state and local, as the latter two also have an impact.

Health-care Providers

Health-care providers supply Sunshine Living with support in the form of medical services. They also impact Sunshine Living's business model by providing client referrals. Having a good reputation with health-care providers is essential to the supply of clients.

Volunteers

Volunteers provide support to the organization for free and are currently a small component of the budget. However, the potential exists here for growth, extending the services that Sunshine Living can provide residents at little to no cost.

Donors

Donors provide funds through donations and bequests, but this is currently a small amount in Sunshine Living's budget because management has not actively pursued this line of income. It has the potential to grow significantly.

Current and Future Business Models

The point here is that many individuals don't understand their own organization's business model.[6] So documenting it in a narrative form, as I've done in the case of Sunshine Living above, has great value to an executive team involved in strategic planning. It helps it to think of the organization as a whole.

But it also greatly benefits such a team in addressing the organization's future, in macro, before getting into the details of strategy design. Exhibit 3.2 summarizes Sunshine Living's current and future situation over the next five years: the planning period in its strategic plan.

Exhibit 3.2   Current and Future Situation

Current	Future
Owners • Current organization size and growth are satisfactory to parent organization, but growth is encouraged.	*Owners* • Grow through opportunistic acquisition of retirement villages and aged-care facilities.
Clients • Retirement living: Demand greater than supply. • Aged care: Running at 99 per cent occupancy rate. • Care-in-the-home: Poorly represented in this part of the industry.	*Clients* • Retirement living: Grow by expanding the number of apartments and townhouses within existing establishments. • Aged care: Grow by expanding the number of rooms within existing establishments. • Care-in-the-home: Expansion opportunity to be grasped.
Staff • Turnover: High turnover of carers in some establishments. • Productivity: Poorly monitored overall.	*Staff* • Turnover: Decrease to cut associated costs. • Productivity: Pockets of low productivity can be improved.
Governments • Federal Government: Funding is formula-driven and is impacted by organization growth.	*Governments* • Federal Government: Organization expansion will drive funds growth.
Health-Care Providers • Access to Sunshine Living's clients drives referrals.	*Health-Care Providers* • Continued access to Sunshine Living will propel growth in referrals.
Volunteers • Currently, volunteer services are unevenly applied across all 17 sites.	*Volunteers* • More volunteer hours to be promoted, thus extending the range of services provided.
Donors • Small amount of funds currently generated from this source.	*Donors* • More funds to be generated in this fashion.

You might note the broad shifts brought on in part by Sunshine Living itself and in part by external forces. The growth in care-in-the-home is a government initiative, for instance. The relationship between these stakeholders and Sunshine Living, and what must happen to reduce cost and propel revenue and profit, is the subject of the organization's business model. Getting it to happen is *strategy*.[7] For instance, what does Sunshine Living need to put in place to grow client revenue and decrease staff turnover or increase volunteer hours – in short, what does it need to do to make its model work? We'll take a look at this in the next chapters.

"Business model" as a concept is relatively new. It has been embraced forcefully in some circles, being seen as a way to engender fresh thinking in the strategy process. I agree with this.

Your Business Model

"Business model" as a concept is relatively new. It has been embraced forcefully in some circles to engender fresh thinking in the strategy process.[8] I agree with this. Keeping discussion initially at a business-model level in strategy sessions enables a CEO, board and management team to take a helicopter view of what their organization does and could do, before descending into detailed discussions. Here are a few pointers to making the process work for you:

Don't Assume. It's been my experience and the observations of others that your directors and management-team members probably don't fully understand your organization's current business model. So, documenting what it is and how it works can be an educational – dare I say enlightening? – experience for them. It will also arm them in developing your organization's strategies.

Plot the New. Considering possible changes and trends – technological, policy-driven, economic and social – determine the likely future situation your organization will face. Embracing or rejecting aspects of that future will shape your business model. But beware of organizational memory, i.e., biases, assumptions and entrenched mindsets that become embedded in organizational systems, as these will hold you back. You may have to unlearn to move on afresh.[9]

Move the "Business." The business model, high tech and the internet go together. But you can extend the concept of "business model" beyond business to government, as I've suggested, and to organizations in the not-for-profit sector, as I've demonstrated. Think broadly when you think "business model."

Don't Forget that Stakeholders Sit Behind Your Business Model. In the previous chapter I stressed the importance of recognizing dependencies. Current and *potential* key stakeholders have a fundamental impact on your organization's performance and underpin its business model. Thinking through the interplay between stakeholders and the business model will help you see how the latter affects the value proposition for each stakeholder group.

Notes

1   The term "business model" has its origins in the mid-1990s and was applied to the impact that the internet was predicted to have on businesses. While the subsequent dot-com crash seemed to assign business-model ideas to the scrap heap, it didn't. The term is now widely applied to how an organization succeeds.

2   See Magretta, J. 2002. Why business models matter. *Harvard Business Review*, May: 86–92; Johnson, M.W., Christensen, C.M. & Kagermann, H. 2008. Reinventing your business model. *Harvard Business Review*, December: 51–59; Mayson, S. 2010. Business models in legal practice. *The College of Law of England and Wales*, March: 1–27.

3   For a discussion on the business-model concept applied to government, see the report by Neely, A. & Delbridge, R. 2007. *Effective business models: What do they mean for Whitehall?* Ascot: Sunningdale Institute.

4   Vijay Govindarajan and Chris Trimble make the point that managerial groups such as these tend to focus on doing what they do better – today's business model – and fail to address the organization's future business model. See, The CEO's role in business model reinvention. *Harvard Business Review*, January–February 2011: 109–114.

5   Joan Magretta makes the excellent point that business models "are, at heart, stories – stories that explain how enterprises work" (p. 87). "When business models don't work, it's because they fail either the narrative test (the story doesn't make sense) or the numbers test (the P&L doesn't add up)" (p. 90). Magretta, J. 2002. Why business models matter. *Harvard Business Review*, May: 86–92.

6   Others have also noted this problem. Mark Johnson, author of *Seizing the white space: Business model innovation for transformative growth and renewal* (Boston: Harvard Business Press, 2010) asks, "Do you know your own business model?" on an online Bloomberg Businessweek Special Report, October 14, 2009. He goes on: "People don't do this intentionally. They don't come to work in the morning saying: 'I'm going to choke off new avenues for growth.' Nor do they come to work saying: 'I'm going to execute my business model.' They probably don't really know their business model. Do you? Can you explicitly describe the value you're delivering to your customers and the precise way in which your company's processes integrate critical resources to deliver that value at a profit? You've likely spent far more time thinking about improving your products to maintain your margins or to attract a younger or more international or otherwise larger target base. In other words, you're focusing on the effect of your business model, not the structure of it." Mark Johnson and his co-authors observe: "Few companies understand their existing business model

well enough – the premise behind its development, its natural interdependencies, and its strengths and limitations. So they don't know when they can leverage their core business and when success requires a new business model." Johnson et al. Reinventing your business model.

7 Ramon Casadesus-Masanell and Joan Ricart put it this way: "Business models refer to the logic of the company – how it operates and captures value for stakeholders in a competitive marketplace; strategy is the plan to create a unique and valuable position involving a distinctive set of activities" (p. 107). How to design a winning business model. *Harvard Business Review*, January–February, 2011: 101–107; see also Seddon, P.B. & Lewis, G.P. 2003. Strategy and business models: What's the difference? *Proceedings of the 7th Pacific Asia Conference on Information Systems*. Adelaide: AIS Electronic Library (AISeL).

8 Govindarajan & Trimble, The CEO's role in business model reinvention.

9 Techniques exist for this undertaking. See, for example, Sinfield, J.V., et al. 2012. How to identify new business models. *MIT Sloan Management Review*: 85–90; Osterwalder, A. & Pigneur, Y. 2010. *Business model generation*. Hoboken: John Wiley & Sons.

Chapter 4

Objectives

Expose Stakeholders in Objectives

Have you ever had this experience? You're in a strategic planning session and the time has come to set *organization* objectives. A member of your group enquires: "What are our objectives?" *Our* doesn't refer to you as managers, of course, but to your organization as a whole. As often happens, the CEO, a senior manager or a professional facilitator will stroll over to a flipchart or whiteboard and write the word "Objectives" on it. Suggestions flow freely, and in no time at all, a large list of items appears.

Over the years, I've looked at these lists and thought "good" and "not so good." The good bit is that the group *has* a list, and everyone has had the opportunity to participate. The not-so-good part is that the process was off the top of peoples' heads, and the resulting list is a real hotchpotch. I've noticed that invariably some items are quantified while others are vague and general. Some are a repeat of the organization's mission, vision and values.

I've looked at these lists and thought there's got to be a better way. And there is. The answers came to me like a series of light bulbs going on in my head – I'd call them flash moments. But first, let's look at a specific example of objective setting gone wrong.

The Wrong Way to Set Objectives

The US Securities and Exchange Commission (SEC) has come under considerable scrutiny and criticism for its role in overseeing the US financial institutions at the center of the Global Financial Crisis, which had its beginning at the end of 2008. I can only speculate about the process it followed to set its objectives, but what the SEC's senior management team produced in its strategic plan is plain to see. The 2004–2009 Plan's first chapter contains its vision, mission and values. Immediately after this, in the same chapter, come its objectives, labeled "goals." The two terms are frequently used interchangeably in management circles, and the SEC doesn't give an additional list specifically labeled objectives. Here is the relevant passage:

DOI: 10.4324/9781003394976-5

To fulfill its mission, the Securities and Exchange Commission will:

- ˙ Enforce compliance with federal securities laws.
- Sustain an effective and flexible regulatory environment.
- Encourage and promote informed investment decision-making; and
- Maximize the use of SEC resources.

These goals are discussed in detail in Chapters Four, Five, Six and Seven.[1]

It's clear to me that nothing in these four statements hasn't already been declared elsewhere. The statements are a rehash of the SEC's vision, mission and values. Without clear and quantified objectives, any old strategy will do. In the US Securities and Exchange Commission's case, when I go to Chapters Four, Five, Six and Seven of its strategic plan, I see assertions about what *staff* are going to *do*, but no strategy! (For another example of objectives that aren't really objectives, see Exhibit 4.1.)

Without clear and quantified objectives, any old strategy will do.

Exhibit 4.1   Nice-to-Haves and Things to Do – But Not Objectives

If executive teams lack an effective method to produce measurable objectives, they usually get together and produce either a jumble of items or bland generalities. Here is one example:

The strategic plan of the Oilseeds Federation was built on "Our Vision," "Our Mission" and "Our Goals." It then follows with "Objectives." There are 14, classified under four headings: Sector Support for Profit; Industry Support/Communication; Market Support; Organizational Capability. Here's a sample of the items:

- Provide leadership across the value chain in addressing issues that serve to impede value creation.
- Increase the proportion of canola meal in the feed ration.
- Promote Australian canola meal to the S.E. Asian markets.
- Provide assurances to stakeholders that market choice is delivered.
- Provide relevant and timely response and actions where issues arise.
- Respond quickly and appropriately to member-raised market access issues.
- Foster appropriate industry segregation protocols for new products.
- Continue to broaden the income base for Australian Oilseeds Federation.[2]

In my observations, with organizations that follow the typical objective-setting process described at the beginning of this chapter, anything goes when it comes to developing strategy. I see strategy developed in a vacuum and sloppy results as a consequence. I see strategy developed without a clear purpose. I see strategy developed without measurable outcomes.

The key to avoiding such a mess is to anchor your objectives to your stakeholders.

Anchoring Objectives to Stakeholders

Let's look at one of the simplest organizations: the convenience store. For its *customers*, there are six strategic factors: range of goods sold; store presentation; location; hours of operation; customer service; and price. Let's suppose I noticed that a particular convenience store had begun to change its presentation and reconfigure itself on the other strategic factors. I might ask the owner, "Why are you doing this?" He might reply, "Because customers have told us we need to modernize, to lift our game." That's a good answer. He might also reply, "Because the competition has made similar changes." While there are traps in simply aping the competition because they might be wrong, it's still not a bad response. If it's grounded in what customers have told him as well, that's fine. But there's still something missing: an *organization* objective.

How does the convenience store manager measure the effectiveness of his changes? This is where a clear and quantified objective comes in. Suppose he goes on to add: "And we want to grow the business by increasing sales by 30 per cent over the next three years." That's an organization objective. It's targeted as well. And it will shape the business's strategy.

The convenience store example leads us to a full-blown method for designing effective and measurable objectives.

The convenience store example leads us to a full-blown method for designing effective and measurable objectives.

By this point, it's doubtless clear that I intend to develop *strategies classified according to key stakeholders*, i.e., strategies for customers, strategies for employees and so on. It might also be plain that measuring these strategies' effectiveness will be a problem if the objectives remain as an undifferentiated set, such as those in Exhibit 4.1.

Flash moment 1: Stakeholders underpin objectives too! The solution I came up with was to classify objectives according to key stakeholders.[3] But I also realized that you can't simply do that as an afterthought with a set of objectives already developed by conventional methods. It won't work. They're in the wrong format and have the wrong content. The steps for developing a set of *measurable* objectives are the focus of this chapter. As Exhibit 4.2 illustrates, by setting objectives according to key stakeholders, we not only have a way to measure each strategy's effectiveness, but we have also established a way to develop a *dimensioned strategy*.

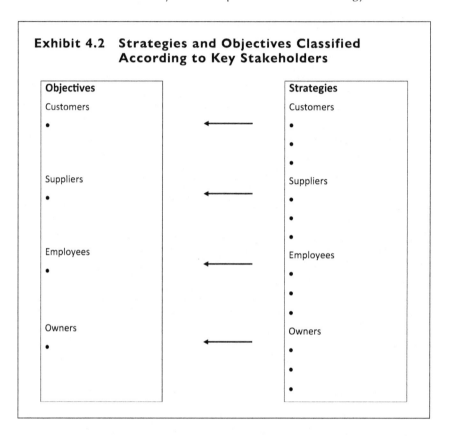

Exhibit 4.2   Strategies and Objectives Classified According to Key Stakeholders

Stakeholders underpin objectives too!

Over many years, as I reviewed the lists of objectives developed conventionally, I noticed a stakeholder pattern in them. It came through with items such as: increasing sales (relates to *customers*); receiving goods in full and on time (*suppliers*); improving productivity and increasing innovation (*employees*); and raising additional capital (*owners*).

Then came flash moment 2: Objectives *for* an organization are also what the organization wants *from* its key stakeholders. This gave me the clue for designing objectives as part of our Strategic Factor System. Objectives express what an organization or business unit wants from its key stakeholders, while strategic factors are what its key stakeholders want from the organization. This is illustrated in Exhibit 4.3, a transformed version of Exhibit 2.1 in Chapter 2. The term "Transactions" in that Exhibit has been replaced by "organization objectives" and "strategic factors."

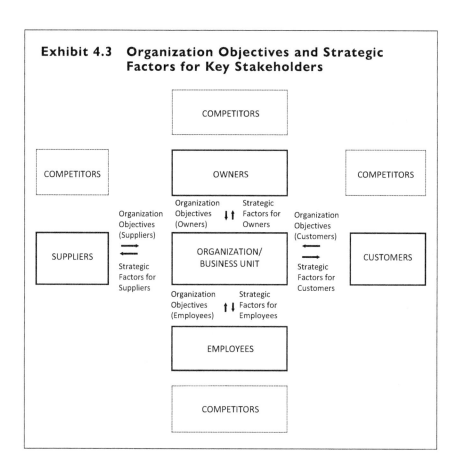

Exhibit 4.3   Organization Objectives and Strategic Factors for Key Stakeholders

---

Objectives *for* an organization are also what the organization wants *from* its key stakeholders.

Defining Desired Behaviors

But we're not there yet. The problem remains: How to develop *measurable* objectives?

Now flash moment 3: Underlying any set of objectives is the desired *behaviors of stakeholders*. We want customers, for example, to buy more from us. We can measure this behavior because it translates into increased sales. So, *behaviors lead to measurable objectives*. To direct the thinking of managers and directors along these lines, I ask: What do you want your customers (or suppliers, or employees, or owners) to *do*?

Underlying any set of objectives is the desired *behaviors of stakeholders*.

The details of the responses can vary enormously, depending on the organization, the industry, the stage of development of a business, etc. The case of a buying group in the food service industry, which I assisted to develop its strategic plan, provides an interesting example of the process in action:

I asked the CEO, who headed up the strategy team of eight: "What do you want your employees to do?" Now admittedly, this is a very broad question. But the CEO wasn't happy with what he was seeing regarding his employees. He had been in the job for 11 months, replacing a CEO who held the position for 15 years.

He answered: "I want them to contribute." A stunned silence followed from the other seven team members, all of whom had been with the company for years.

Eventually, the Financial Controller protested, "You can't put that down. That would imply that they don't contribute already."

So, I probed further: "What do you mean by 'contribute'?" I asked the CEO.

"Well," he said, "since I've been here, I've noticed that people stick pretty much to their jobs. They're not forthcoming with ideas. They don't seem to be engaged in the business. It's as if the last CEO drove all initiative out of the staff."

Considerable debate followed this statement as to how much time and effort the business should expect from its staff, what form "contributing" might take, the staff's different personalities and cultural backgrounds, and so on. But I finally got the CEO to enunciate that what he and the buying group wanted from the employees was "to be more innovative." That was the behavioral outcome. The team could now proceed to fashion an organization objective, with targets, and move on to formulate strategies for the employees, one of its key stakeholders.

I always take management teams and boards back to this initial level of describing desired behavioral outcomes so they can clearly stipulate what they want to happen. I aim to avoid getting lost in detail and caught up in word-mongering, which, ultimately, produces confusion. And it works! Teams are forced to be *clear*. After we have pinned down the behavioral outcomes we want from stakeholders, we move to setting objectives. (Organizations are continually in this ebb and flow of influencing stakeholder behavior – see Exhibit 4.4.)

Exhibit 4.4   Responding to, or Modifying, the Stakeholder

It's a truism that organizations need to respond to customers' or stakeholders' needs. Like all taken-for-granteds, it isn't always that simple. Organizations of all types are also in the process of grooming their stakeholders.

They start by first choosing those that best suit them – the "targets." Then they try to get them to do what the organization wants. For example, retail businesses want to shift customers over to their high-margin lines and away from their low-margin ones. Microsoft wants its customers to move to its latest products and abandon its old ones. Banks are pushing consumers to go online to cut transaction costs. Manufacturers are continually influencing suppliers to re-engineer and smooth their supply chains. In local government, the push has been on, globally, to have ratepayers recycle their waste.

Systems and incentives have been put in place to achieve these goals. All of these are desired *behavioral outcomes* but, crucially, they have been developed within the broad scope of stakeholder needs.

Developing *Measurable* Objectives

It's general practice to write objectives this way: "To increase sales…; to decrease injuries…; to maintain funds…" I have kept that style of expression in designing objectives.

To take an example, in the case of an investment advisory and funds management group with high employee turnover, the behavior desired of employees was "To get quality employees to join the organization and stay." This morphed into the objective: "To decrease employee turnover," and measures and targets were set around this. The quality of the employees was to be controlled at intake and hence to become a given.

Now we come to measurement, and here, I noticed, was another place where management teams and boards stumble and fall. There's great confusion over what a measure is. Wouldn't it be great, I thought, if we could come up with a simple discipline, even a set of symbols, which, if applied, would result in individuals automatically designing real measures?

Flash moment 4: $, #, %

I noticed that some measures involved numbers, e.g., number of units produced, number of patients, number of defects, number of days late and so on. So, I designated a symbol, #, to mean "number of," with which to start these measures. Thus, the measures became: # units produced, # patients, etc.

I also became aware of another group of measures that concerned dollars, or the local currency. So, I introduced another symbol to clarify that we were dealing with a measure. Thus, dollars saved from process improvements, dollar revenue, dollar profit, etc., becomes: $ saved from process improvements, $ revenue, $ profit...

These two symbols covered quite a range of measures and introduced some necessary discipline into the measurement process. But I realized there was one more commonly occurring measure type: "%." Many measures require a percentage. Examples include: % market share; % customer satisfaction with service; % share of funds from government; % debt/equity ratio and so on. As a result, "%" became the third symbol introduced into my system. (The measure "% points" is also covered by the symbol "%.")

Together these three symbols – $, #, % – cover all measures. Any item that can't have one of these symbols sitting comfortably in front of it isn't a measure. This discipline has worked beautifully to avoid having actions, program descriptions and nice-to-haves listed as measures.

Together these three symbols – $, #, % – cover all measures. Any item that can't have one of these symbols sitting comfortably in front of it isn't a measure.

Objectives Reveal "Key" Stakeholders

Let me now share with you what occurred in one objective-setting process I facilitated within a national law firm of over 600 staff. It illustrates how this process invariably highlights precisely who the *key* stakeholders are.

The strategic planning team numbered around 30 people, including the Managing Partner; all the other Partners; State Managers (some of whom were also Partners); seven Board Directors (who were also Partners); other lawyers; and non-legal staff (such as the Chief Operating Officer, the Human Resources Manager and the Financial Controller). The board and senior management had decided to involve such a large group to bring in a diversity of opinions and ensure commitment to the completed strategic plan.

Early in the initial workshop, while we were still working as one large group, I asked: "Who are your *key* stakeholders?"

"Clients," came the clear response. "Employees" and "Partners" also received consensus.

So, I put these three on the whiteboard and asked: "Are there any others?"

"The community," a few people said. I asked the whole group if I should add "community" to the list, and most agreed. But I wasn't convinced. Who is the community? I thought. This seems pretty vague. I didn't want to confront my concerns immediately, however, and hoped that by defining "clients," "employees," and "partners," it would become clear who exactly the "community" was.

The group and I discussed "clients" – not just *current* clients but also *potential* clients, i.e., clients who are now with the competition. In addition, we considered *non-clients*, individuals and organizations that wouldn't dream of going to any large, city-based law firm with their legal problems. We also discussed how objectives and strategies might differ for these sub-groups. We reviewed "employees" and "partners" in a similar way, also considering potential employees and potential partners in addition to the current ones.

Finally, I had to return to the term "community" and express my doubts about it as a *key* stakeholder. It's easy to throw items onto a whiteboard, but they must pass the key-stakeholder tests outlined in Exhibit 2.3, Chapter 2. "What makes the community a *key* stakeholder for *your* law firm?" I asked. "You've covered a fair bit of the community already with clients, current and potential, non-clients, and employees, current and potential. Who's left that's relevant? What do you want from the community? What do you want it to do?"

As you will recognize, these two final questions are concerned with behavioral outcomes. The answers to them were meant to lead the law firm's team to design measurable objectives – which was a necessary step if they were to develop a precise strategy for the community, not just some woolly ideas.

The group couldn't answer my questions. So, I expanded: "Is your relationship with the community strategic or operational?" After more blank looks, I continued. "It's *operational* if you give a certain percentage of firm profit to the community and expect nothing in return – just as you and I might give money to the Salvation Army or Red Cross. We expect nothing in return. But if your firm is providing funds to the community and expecting something in return, then the relationship is *strategic* – and you need to develop a strategy around 'community.'"

I must admit that until this point, I'd never articulated this view about stakeholders quite so clearly, i.e., if you can't state what you want *from* a stakeholder, the relationship isn't strategic – and it's probably not a *key* stakeholder.

If you can't state what you want *from* a stakeholder, then the relationship isn't strategic – and it's probably not a *key* stakeholder.

Did I get an answer to my questions: What do you want from the community? What do you want it to do? Well, yes and no. One of the firm's Partners suggested that supporting the community was "a ticket to play the game." By this he meant that by supporting community causes, the firm became eligible for membership in government panels of law firms, from which firms are invited to provide quotations for government work. Supporting the community was a prerequisite. Now, I thought, that's *strategic*. But the precise relationship the law firm has with the community and its objective relative to the community remained a work in progress. Exhibit 4.5 is an extract from the firm's strategic plan, the section concerned with organization objectives. You will note the absence of "community."

Exhibit 4.5   Law Firm: Extract of Objectives, Measures and Targets

Behavioral Outcome	Organization Objective	Measure	Target
Clients			
- to get current clients to remain with us and purchase more of our range of services across all offices	- to increase profitable revenue from existing clients	• $ revenue, existing clients • $ profit, existing clients	$91 million $18 million
Clients			
- to get potential clients and non-clients to buy our services and products	- to increase profitable revenue from new clients	• $ revenue, new clients • $ profit, new clients	$10 million $2 million
Employees			
- to get quality employees to join the organization and stay	- to decrease employee turnover	• % employee turnover	10%
Partners			
- to get partners to contribute to the prosperity of the firm in an equitable way	- to increase partner contribution	• # minimum partner hours contributed • $ minimum partner supervised fee base	2,200 $1.6 million

As Exhibit 4.5 shows, from measures, we move to targets. When it comes to target setting, A.G. Lafley, the CEO of Proctor & Gamble (P&G) for nine years, has an important message for us all in Exhibit 4.6.

Exhibit 4.6   On Target Setting

A.G. Lafley became CEO of P&G in June 2000, remaining in that position until 2009. During that period, P&G rose on the Fortune 500 list from 31st largest in sales and 22nd largest in profit, to 20th in sales and 9th in profit. Sales per employee grew from $363,000 in 2000 to $585,000 in 2009. Profit per employee increased from $32,000 to $84,000 over the same period. He provides this illuminating perspective on target setting:

> At P&G we had gotten into the habit of treating internal stretch goals as external commitments. Once a company starts pursuing unrealistic growth objectives, it will rarely, if ever, create the capability and flexibility to invest in long-term growth. Instead, it will borrow from the future to sustain the present – pulling volume from the next quarter to deliver in the current quarter, for example. The result is few resources and increasingly limited latitude to make investments in the future. Before establishing P&G's long-term goals, I had to decide what would be "good enough" to deliver in the short term. Early on as CEO, I announced that we were reducing our goals. The stock price increased more than 8% as investors recognized that our lower goals were realistic, and we were making the right decision for the long term. Although we've often exceeded our targets, we've resisted pressure to raise them above what makes sense.[4]

Stakeholders, Objectives and the Public Company

Wesfarmers, Australia's eighth-largest company by market capitalization, can provide a demonstration of the thinking that goes on behind objective setting in large public companies. Wesfarmers is highly diversified and very successful.[5] It describes its purpose thus:

> Wesfarmers has become well known for its focus on providing satisfactory returns to shareholders – our long-established primary objective.

[Note the word "satisfactory," not "maximum" here.]... we deal with a broad range of issues directly linked to business success. These include the nature of our relationships with our employees, customers and suppliers and our interaction with the physical environment and the communities in which we operate. We have an obligation to provide safe workplaces for all our employees and that will always be a key priority for Wesfarmers. As well as being safe, we aim to make the working environment as satisfying and rewarding an experience as possible ... Supplying customers with quality goods and a second-to-none service level is vital to our ongoing success, as is the need for our employees to act honestly and ethically in all their business dealings. With respect to the environment, the extremely diverse nature of our operations, both geographically and in terms of industry and business sectors, requires constant vigilance to maintain the highest possible standards. Wesfarmers puts a lot of effort into getting these things right. We must continue to do so and continue our proud record of community support if we are to ensure that, in all respects, we operate in a truly sustainable way.[6]

With this sustainability philosophy in place, Wesfarmers' management team and board goes about *getting the settings right* for all key stakeholders, including shareholders, to enhance the chances of long-term survival. This means working out what the company needs from its key stakeholders as inputs and what it needs to accomplish in strategy and action terms to obtain them. This is illustrated in Exhibit 4.7 and demonstrated in the following quote from Wesfarmers' then CEO, Richard Goyder.

"Of course, we want to make a dollar," Goyder says. "But we want to do that in a way that is ethical and responsible. That means making sure that our employees have a safe place to work and opportunities to develop. It means treating the environment with respect. It means dealing appropriately with our customers and suppliers. And it means supporting and benefiting the communities in which we operate." Integrity, he continues, is everything: "Without integrity it would be impossible to remain competitive over the medium-to-long term. Customers and suppliers won't deal with you if you don't have values they think you should have. Our view is that if you compromise on your ethics, then you've got nothing. Once you've lost trust, the game's over."[7]

Wesfarmers demonstrates the true picture of business life: trade-offs, compromises, but, ultimately, settings and targets. From my experience, Goyder also demonstrates an accurate picture of life in the not-for-profit and public sectors. In other words, managing organizations in these other sectors also involves trade-offs, compromise and an awful lot of juggling. I work in all three sectors – private, public and not-for-profit – and looking through a firm-centric-stakeholder lens, I note that they are more alike than each would care to acknowledge.

Exhibit 4.7   Survival Linked to Strategies and Actions

Maximizing the probability of long-term survival of the organization

Achieving required inputs from stakeholders

(e.g., revenue from customers, funds from owners,

effort from employees – "organization objectives")

Performing well on strategic factors for stakeholders

(i.e., effective strategies and actions for customers,

owners, employees, etc.)

So, what do CEOs, executive teams and boards maximize, if anything? The only thing I can put my finger on in all cases is the organization's long-term survival probability.[8] This involves systemic design – molding objectives and working with stakeholders to achieve them, thus sustaining the organization for the long haul.

This involves systemic design – molding objectives and working with stakeholders to achieve them, thus sustaining the organization for the long haul.

Your Objectives – the Effective Way

It's likely that you have found the objective-setting process a nightmare involving disputes over definitions and style, rather than substance. You may have also experienced a jumble of declarations that are impossible to link directly to strategy statements:

Unlearn to Re-Learn. Your first step is to unlearn to re-learn. You need to approach the task of objective setting with an open mind and think differently about the task ahead.

Stakeholders in Focus. Focus again on stakeholders. It must be becoming very clear by now that I advocate structuring everything you do in strategy around your stakeholders. They're your foundation stones in objective setting too.

Behavioral Outcomes. It may at first appear to be an unusual step: to work out what you want your stakeholders to do for your organization. But it works. I've supplied you with a style of wording to employ. Following that will make life simpler. These behavioral outcomes must be clear and complete. I suggest one per stakeholder group.

Objectives. Convert the behavioral outcomes you have identified into objectives for your organization or business unit. Again, I've provided a format here, which you'll find won't act as a constraint – quite the contrary. It will free you to think "content" rather than "style" and "form."

Measures and Targets. Design measures and targets on these objectives by cycling through $, # and %. Ask: "Are there any $ ways we can measure that?" And after noting responses, ask about # and % ways. You'll find that this method induces participants to think of real "measures" rather than spurious items such as actions by individuals that sometimes fall under the measure category. Next, before designing strategy, set targets stakeholder group by stakeholder group on the shortlist of measures you've drawn out from the previous step.

Cause and Effect. Without a clear line from strategies (means) to objectives (ends), "anything goes." Your strategic planning sessions should not become a series of anchorless arguments in which status and personality prevail over logic. And they won't if you follow the process outlined in this chapter. It's a well-articulated method to establish clear and measurable objectives for your organization or business unit. It breaks through the prevailing wordy and confusing approaches and leads the way to clear and purposeful strategy.

Notes

1 US Securities and Exchange Commission, 2004. *2004 Performance and Accountability Report*. Washington: SEC, p. 9. www.sec.gov/about/secpar/secpar04.pdf
2 Australian Oilseeds Federation, 2013. *Annual Report 2012–13*, p. 4.
3 Igor Ansoff discussed objective setting in his pioneering text, *Corporate Strategy*, but rejected early "stakeholder theory" because, as he wrote, "the theory maintains that the objectives of the firm should be derived by balancing the conflicting claims of the various 'stakeholders' in the firm: managers, workers, stockholders, suppliers, vendors" (p. 39). In this interpretation, *organization* objectives become what stakeholders want *from* the firm. In his rejection, Ansoff failed to pick up that organization objectives are what the firm, as an entity, wants *from* a stakeholder group in order to prosper. Thus objectives to do with profitable revenue are based on obtaining this *from* the stakeholder, that is,

customers. Objectives concerned with improving productivity and increasing innovation are what a firm wants *from* another set of stakeholders, i.e., employees. And so it goes. Ansoff, H.I. 1965. *Corporate strategy*. New York: McGraw Hill. For more from Ansoff, see 1979. *Strategic management*. London: Macmillan, and 1984. *Implanting strategic management*. Englewood Cliffs: Prentice Hall. For a full review of the academic literature on "organizational aspirations, reference points and goals," see Shinkle, G.A. 2012. Organizational aspirations, reference points and goals: Building on the past and aiming for the future. *Journal of Management*, 38: 415–455.

4 A.G. Lafley, 2009. What only the CEO can do. *Harvard Business Review*, May: 54–62, p. 60.

5 Wesfarmers was one of the successful diversifiers presented in my book, *Diversification Blueprint: Managing in a Diversified Organization*, published in Australia in 2008 by President Press and republished in 2009 in the rest of the world by Kogan Page as *Diversification Strategy: How to Grow a Business by Diversifying Successfully*.

6 Wesfarmers' 2005 *Annual Report*: 10–11.

7 Morgan, S. 2006. Blueprint for success. *Management Today*, October, p. 8.

8 As Drucker has put it in answer to his own question: "What should these objectives be, then? There is only one answer: Objectives are needed in every area where performance and results directly and vitally affect the survival and prosperity of the business." Drucker, P.F. 1955. *The practice of management*. London: Pan Books.

Chapter 5

Competitive Advantage

Divulge Strategy's Dirty Secret

When I first started as a consultant running my public seminars on strategic planning, all I had as frameworks were Michael Porter's generic strategies and the beginnings of our "Strategic Factors" method. In his various publications, Michael Porter, the Harvard Business School based Professor of Strategy, distinguishes between two basic types of competitive advantage: lower cost and differentiation.[1] This framework has influenced many managers' thinking and can be found in numerous textbooks. But after thinking it through and applying it, I wasn't sure I could go with it. I returned to this basic question: What is competitive advantage?

I came to the view that to define competitive advantage effectively, I had to take an external frame of reference and stick with it. It's a reference point I describe as "outside-in": viewing an organization from the outside looking in, *not* from the inside looking out. Approaching competitive advantage and differentiation in this way made it impossible for me to see "lower cost" as anything other than a change in the frame of reference. Through the lower-cost lens I'm looking at competitive advantage not from the *outside-in*, as I do with differentiation, but from the *inside-out* – not from the customer's point of view but from the organization's. This shift converted competitive advantage into an internal *operations* concept. And operational efficiency, while important and capable of improving profits by cutting costs, is not *competitive* strategy.

I came to the view that to define competitive advantage effectively, I had to take an external frame of reference and stick with it.

All of this left me with the following conclusion: an organization achieves competitive advantage by differentiating itself on the strategic factors relevant to its key stakeholders; customers are one stakeholder and price is one of those factors. The organization takes a position on these factors and delivers superior *value* in the eyes of the stakeholder. However, it can only

DOI: 10.4324/9781003394976-6

sustain its position through operational efficiency, one form of which is achieving low cost. To maximize long-term success, however it's measured, a firm must produce an effective strategy *and* achieve lower cost. But lower cost is *not*, in itself, competitive strategy.

An organization achieves competitive advantage by differentiating itself on the strategic factors relevant to its key stakeholders.

As you've just witnessed, I have struggled with strategy. I'm fairly certain you have, too. (Exhibit 5.1 provides more examples of the struggle.)[2]

The Slider

At a basic level you no doubt have a feel for what strategy is. It captures the ideas of maneuvering, obtaining advantage and plotting. As you dig deeper, though, you may find that it becomes confused with planning, objectives, goals, targets and even actions by individuals – as we've seen in Exhibit 5.1. In no time at all, you join many others totally confused by "strategy."

I found that in my public seminars and consulting I needed a metaphor to capture the essence of strategy and to explain positioning.

Most of us are familiar with the volume control on a computer. It's a slider that we move from left to right or top to bottom. Left is low volume, and right can be pretty loud. I regard strategy as sliding the "volume control" on a strategic factor from left to right or vice versa, to find the right *position*.

McDonald's response to its rare growth-and-profit hiccup provides an excellent illustration of the slider in operation.

In 2002, McDonald's had 30,000 restaurants in more than 100 countries, with 1.6 million store employees serving 47 million customers daily. Yet, results faltered after more than 35 years of non-stop growth since its stock market float in 1965. Between 1997 and 2003, its fast-food market share fell by 3 per cent. The Board was forced to concede that it had a problem and replaced its CEO. The new chief, Jim Cantalupo, who had previously held the role, re-focused the business and returned to basics. The result for 2003 was a profit close to $1.5 billion, with global sales increasing by nearly 11 per cent over the previous year. By early 2004, sales growth had leapt by 24 per cent over the 2002 level. As a result, from 2002 to 2004, McDonald's share price doubled. The company has powered along ever since.[3]

McDonald's has focused on changes to at least four strategic factors for *customers*, as shown in Exhibit 5.2. It slid the control on *product range* to the right. The company wasn't giving customers what they wanted, so they expanded their product range by adding Salads Plus and chicken; by

Exhibit 5.1 Strategy Confusion

I sometimes ask my seminar audiences to write an example of a strategy. The group usually comprises board members and senior and middle managers from medium-to-large organizations in the private, public and not-for-profit sectors. They often hold degrees in various disciplines and occupy positions such as Director, CEO, Managing Director, General Manager, Financial Controller, Marketing Manager, Sales Manager, Operations Manager and so on. Many have MBAs. There are no names on the answer sheets for what becomes an obvious reason: the results are highly embarrassing to all participants.

If there are 25 people in the room – the maximum we allow – there will be 25 different strategy examples, and rarely do I receive even *one* that qualifies as a true strategy. Yet each and every one of these managers and directors talk "strategy" all the time. I point out to my audience that this same variation exists *within* their management teams and boards and *across* their organizations. Their jaws drop. With this brief exercise, they realize the battle they face in designing a successful *strategic* plan.

Below are some sample responses. The list contains what might be labeled goals, objectives, actions and vague statements of intent. Only the last one comes close to a genuine example of a strategy.

- "Growth."
- "Engage sales outlets."
- "Devise advertising program."
- "To achieve superior operational outcomes through efficient and effective work practices."
- "To become competitive in an existing architectural market."
- "Increase product 'x' sales by 70 per cent in a two-year period to take market leadership."
- "Attract, retain and develop capable people."
- "An expansion of our work into the Asia-Pacific region."
- "Optimize return on investments."
- "Develop a service delivery model incorporating tactical projects."
- "Set our charges at a level that makes us competitive with our competitors in the industry."

providing an in-store coffee and cakes selection via McCafe; and by supplying different options for beef burgers. Firms often narrow their range
when under pressure, but McDonald's broadened theirs, and today it
includes items such as the Angus Beef Burger as a premium item.[4] (This
varies by country these days.)

Regarding the change to its strategy setting on product range, McDonald's CEO for Australia, Peter Bush, had this to say: "The revamping of the
menu has been a crucial part of the McDonald's strategy over the past
seven or eight years. Consumer habits have been changing. They wanted
more variety, and they wanted more options. They want one end of the
spectrum to the other – burger to salads."[5]

On *image* and *store presentation*, McDonald's also moved its slider
considerably – to the right. On *image*, it shook off the obesity and high-fat

**Exhibit 5.2   McDonald's Strategy Settings and
Statements on Four Strategic Factors
for Customers**

Strategic Factor	Strategy Setting		Strategy Statements
Product range	⇩ → ⇩ Low High		Position on *product range*: Include McCafe, salads, a wider choice of nutritional foods, in addition to traditional products.
Image	⇩ → ⇩ Low High		Position on *image*: Contemporary and a provider of healthy food.
Store presentation	⇩ → ⇩ Low High		Position on *store presentation*: In keeping with image, incorporate a more current appearance, different seating arrangements, features and colors.
Price	⇩ Low High		Position on *price*: A competitive level with alternative restaurants and consistent with positions on other strategic factors.

label via effective advertising, in-store nutritional information and product labeling. In the US, it removed super sizes from its drinks range. On *store presentation*, it modernized, changing the layout, seating arrangements and colors and included additional features, such as wireless internet connections and plasma TV screens. On *price*, McDonald's held its ground, not moving the volume control at all, with no significant price increases at that time. Instead, the premium products in its product range increased average customer spend. Customers had more products to choose from, they liked the stores, they liked the prices and they spent more. Getting the settings right on all *strategic factors* for its current, potential and lapsed customers produced a *competitive advantage* for McDonald's because it yielded superior *value* for customers, i.e., price weighted against the company's performance on all other strategic factors.

Strategy vs. Action

As we've witnessed previously, strategy gets confused with mission and vision statements, goals, etc.[6] But a major blockage for managers is the lack of clarity regarding the difference between *strategy* and *action*. Time and again, I pick up strategic plans expecting to see strategy, and I only get – action. Why?

Time and again, I pick up strategic plans expecting to see strategy, and I only get – action.

The answer is extremely important and concerns the *level of analysis*. In one form, this is how we explain behavior. Let's look at a very different example: 16-year-old Johnnie's bad behavior. One explanation is that Johnnie behaves as he does because it's his personality – an individual-level explanation. No, someone else suggests, it's not his personality, it's his family's background – a family-level explanation. Another explanation suggests is it's his peer group – a neighborhood-level explanation. And so it goes.

This level-of-analysis problem snares management teams when they come to write strategy. They think that strategy is an individual-level phenomenon, not an organization-level one. There's a vast difference, for example, between McDonald's positions on its strategic factors for customers (Exhibit 5.2) and what employees within McDonald's need to do to implement them. Often there is a level missing and a great hole in the strategic plan. As a result, there is little chance that issues concerning competitive advantage will be addressed. (See Exhibit 5.3 for tips on how to recognize a *strategic* plan.)

Exhibit 5.3   Spot the Difference: *Strategic* **Plan vs.** *Operational* **Plan**

Managers and directors clearly struggle to distinguish between a strategic plan and an operational one. A strategic decision externally repositions an organization in some way, i.e., changing its competitiveness in its marketplace through decisions on things like product range, price, store presentation and customer service.

For example, a bank's senior management team and board might decide to close a particular branch and instead serve customers online. Clearly, this is a strategic decision because it affects the bank's competitiveness in that region on the strategic factor of location.

An operational decision, by contrast, takes the organization's position in the marketplace as given and develops ways to implement that position. A bank branch, for example, makes operational decisions only as the strategic decisions have already been taken at other higher levels. Operational decisions pertain to *efficiency* rather than *competitiveness*. The bank branch's operational plan is concerned with achieving the bank's desired levels of customer service, for example, as efficiently as possible, e.g., management decides to create lounge areas for loan application discussions or demonstrates online banking to local customers, so they don't need to come into the branch so often.

There should be only a few written strategic plans in a large, multi-divisional organization, one per division, and only one strategic plan in a small-to-medium-sized enterprise. *All* other plans are operational.

Positions, Not Actions

Writing strategy is difficult because it requires the members of a strategy team to think at a level above what is natural. The natural level is that of the individual, you and me, and what we're going to do. This is *action*. The team must think on the organization level and envisage organization *positions*. Hence a familiar debate begins: "Is that a strategy?" "Looks like an objective to me." "Isn't that an action?" And so it goes.

To avoid this wheel-spinning, I've developed a strict format for strategy statements. Let's look at it in relation to McDonald's strategy settings in Exhibit 5.2. Each statement in the exhibit describes the position the company designed for itself on each of four strategic factors to achieve its competitive advantage.

The *first* important feature to note in the format and style of these statements is that they're positions, not actions.

The *second* feature of note in good strategy statements is that the position is described on a *strategic factor*, which I have highlighted in italics. This focuses attention on competitive advantage and prevents managers from leaping into action prematurely. In the case of another client, a producer of software for payroll systems, I found that managers were only too ready to tell all assembled what needed doing, i.e., activity. It was only by channeling this energy to address the company's required positions on *strategic factors* that we avoided producing a no-strategy plan.

The *third* feature is the description of the position taken. It may be brief, i.e., one sentence or a short paragraph. Care has to be taken here to avoid writing down the actions that will follow the position itself. McDonald's position on product range called for actions concerned with training staff, installing new equipment and sourcing new suppliers. These rightly belong in the action list, *not* in the strategy statement itself.

Since competitors play an important role in strategy design, the chosen position on a strategic factor is a function of what a key stakeholder wants *and* the position taken, or likely to be taken, by competitors. McDonald's, for example, also reviewed its competitors' positions on product range, image, store presentation and price in coming to its positions on these factors.

The chosen position on a strategic factor is a function of what a key stakeholder wants, *and* the position taken, or likely to be taken, by competitors.

Developing a Competitive Advantage Profile

Rustic (not its real name), a finance company, illustrates the process you might go through in positioning your organization on strategic factors.

Rustic's customers are mainly farmers. In fact, 80 per cent of its revenue comes from them, with the remainder derived from rural businesses. I had been chosen to conduct Rustic's Strategy Workshop, which was to take place over a day and a half. There were 25 managers and directors in attendance. My role was to steer the group through an agreed agenda that I had designed in conjunction with the Managing Director and the General Manager of Finance and Administration. The workshop participants were the Managing Director, six non-executive directors, business-unit managers and field sales staff. My aim as facilitator was to help the team identify Rustic's existing competitive advantage and steer them through a series of steps to raise its competitiveness even further.

The first session took place on the afternoon of day one. We discussed customers, and the group zeroed in on farmers since, as I've said, this was the source of 80 per cent of Rustic's business. Serving farmers' needs was seen as the primary reason for the company's existence. I raised the question: What *are* the strategic factors for farmers?

I then presented the group with a draft list that I had earlier developed via a separate meeting involving the General Manager of Finance and Administration, the Manager of Human Resources and myself. At that meeting, we had also developed definitions of each strategic factor *by taking a farmer's perspective* as best we could. The list appears in Exhibit 5.4. I was concerned that the three of us might have gotten it wrong or that it might be incomplete, given that the group was composed of only the two people from head office and me.

The large group of 25 debated:

- Whether the strategic factors we had identified were the right ones.
- Whether they were precisely defined from a *farmer's point of view*.

With 25 people, I was given many opinions and numerous suggestions. I was grateful for them, especially those from the field sales staff, whom I saw as being most in touch with the farmers and their expectations. But I was having trouble amalgamating the views of 25 participants. So, at afternoon tea, about an hour and a half into the session, I suggested that a sub-group of four be formed to pull the various opinions together and produce a second draft of the strategic factors and their definitions. The large team agreed this was a good idea and decided that the sub-group should include the original three people – the General Manager of Finance and Administration, the Manager of Human Resources and me – plus the Managing Director.

It took the four of us about half an hour to complete a redraft of the strategic factors and their definitions based on the larger group's input. After the break, the Managing Director presented the new list to the group. Further debate and amendments followed until the group agreed on a final list of strategic factors, with their definitions. During this discussion every attempt was made, as I have said, to take a typical farmer's view. The result is in Exhibit 5.5.

Note the differences between Exhibits 5.4 and 5.5. The revised list contains two additional factors: "customer relationship" and "community involvement." These had been overlooked by the original small group and second small sub-group and were introduced because of the larger group's broader knowledge of farmers and their expectations. The definition of "customer service" was also expanded and refined. The group thought that

Exhibit 5.4   Strategic Factors for Rustic's Customers – First Draft

Price
- Interest rate
- Fees

Expertise
- Farm/business knowledge
- Financial knowledge
- Educational level of staff

Customer Service
- On-farm visits
- Follow-up service regarding variations
- Handling customer inquiries
- Flexibility of services, including online facilities
- Customer relationship

Range of Products
- Loan options
- Ability to switch and tailor products

Mortgage Security
- Per cent of assets mortgaged

Company Image
- Secure future of company
- Length of time in the industry
- Peer opinion
- Office presentation
- Brand identification

Accessibility
- Location of offices
- Availability of field officers

part of the definition – "customer relationship," on the original list – was vague, so it was changed and expanded to "confidentiality of the relationship" and "response times to inquiries and loan processing." I noticed how the field sales staff played a significant role in clarifying and modifying the definition of "customer service."

Exhibit 5.5   Strategic Factors for Rustic's Customers – Workshop Draft

Price
- Interest rate
- Fees

Expertise
- Farm/business knowledge
- Financial knowledge
- Educational level of staff

Customer Service
- On-farm visits
- Follow-up service regarding variations
- Handling customer inquiries
- Flexibility of services, including online facilities
- Confidentiality of the relationship
- Response times to inquiries and loan processing

Range of Products
- Loan options
- Ability to switch and tailor products

Mortgage Security
- Per cent of assets mortgaged

Company Image
- Secure future of company
- Length of time in the industry
- Peer opinion
- Office presentation
- Brand identification

Accessibility
- Location of offices
- Availability of field officers

Customer Relationship
- Long-term support
- Riding the bumps with clients
- Understanding rural issues
- Stability of relationship with staff

Community Involvement
- Agricultural shows
- Donations/scholarships/sponsorships/field days
- Industry networks

The three of us who had met before this large workshop had also prepared a *draft* of what I call a Competitive Advantage Profile. It listed the *net* advantages of Rustic over competitors, which are labeled Other Rural Lenders. This table was now the subject of serious debate and amendment. We had to add the two new strategic factors to the analysis: customer relationship and community development. Following much discussion, the team of 25 agreed on a final amended version of the Competitive Advantage Profile. This is shown in Exhibit 5.6.

You can see that the listed *net* advantages are based on the definitions of the strategic factors in Exhibit 5.5. The reason for "net" is that if Rustic and its competitors perform equally well on a factor, the resultant advantage is "nil." If there's a difference, we note that. For example, under Expertise, Rustic provided two things better than Other Rural Lenders: "better farm/business knowledge" and "all field staff tertiary educated." On the other side, Other Rural Lenders provided nil services better than Rustic.

Of course, there is a shortcoming in Rustic's method. All this analysis is based on management's knowledge of its farmers. The farmers themselves aren't undertaking the assessments. But Rustic's field sales staff, who visit farmers regularly, were present. They have more than a fair knowledge of farmers' strategic factors, their definitions and Rustic's performance on them. Despite this, Rustic's management resolved to verify these factors, their definitions and the performance assessments over time. Via this process, it was Rustic's intent to transfer certain net advantages from the right column to the left in Exhibit 5.6.

Exhibit 5.6   Competitive Advantage Profile for Customers of Rustic

Rustic (Net Advantages)	Other Rural Lenders (Net Advantages)
Price • No ongoing fees and charges	**Price** • Will discount interest rates to obtain business • Will discount fees to win business
Expertise • Better farm/business knowledge • All field staff tertiary educated	**Expertise** • Nil
Customer Service • On-farm visits • Easier access to office staff • Better follow-up service and handling of inquiries	**Customer Service** • Nil
Range of Products • Nil	**Range of Products** • Greater range, including checkbooks, credit cards, leasing, etc. • Whole of finance service
Mortgage Security • Nil	**Mortgage Security** • Less stringent
Company Image • Better image • Not seen as cross-seller	**Company Image** • Less conservative image than Rustic, e.g., more generous in assessment
Accessibility • Better access to decision-makers	**Accessibility** • Greater spread of offices
Customer Relationships • Rustic "rides the bumps" with clients • Stability of relationship with staff	**Customer Relationships** • Nil
Community Involvement • Stronger involvement	**Community Involvement** • Nil

Research Always Needed

Rustic's case clearly demonstrates the importance of understanding the customer's or other stakeholders' experience. I've found that managers are often way off-beam when it comes to what customers or other stakeholders really want and where to focus strategy. Here's one example.

I've found that managers are often way off-beam when it comes to what customers or other stakeholders really want and where to focus strategy.

Pete is the Managing Director of a public company I'll call Callard Holdings, which imports gift products, mainly from Asian countries such as China and Indonesia. It also manufactures clothing items and exports products overseas. Its products are mainly of the gift "variety" type, which includes calendars, homewares such as cups and drinking mugs, greeting cards, sports trading cards, confectionery and clothing. The clothing items include T-shirts, boxer shorts, socks, caps and the like. They're all low-end, low-priced items.

Callard Holdings' customers are retail stores located in shopping malls and residential shopping areas, as well as the giftware sections of large department stores. The company doesn't sell directly to individuals, but its products are distributed nationwide.

I was involved in helping Pete and his management team develop a strategic plan for the company. During the sessions, it emerged that Pete was quite convinced that the way to grow company sales was to generate "brand loyalty" among consumers – individuals who were the retailers' customers. His idea was to mark all products with Callard's brand, even if they already had a manufacturer's sticker or tag, which was the case with many products, such as drinking mugs. From his remote Managing Director's desk, Pete's view was that over time, customers would look to buy "Callard" products, and the company would thus increase market share.

As part of the strategic planning, my company was asked to undertake market research for Callard Holdings to identify the strategic factors for its customers, the retailers. So, we drew up a schedule and set about conducting 16 interviews with retail store owners and department store buyers. After one of our staff had completed just 12 interviews, a clear pattern emerged. The retailers chose Callard over its competitors because of its performance on the strategic factors: customer service, delivery, price range at retail, retail profit margin, product range and the packaging/presentation of the products themselves. The additional four interviews only confirmed what the previous 12 had already told us.

Several other questions were, of course, asked during the interviews, including whether retailers thought that Callard Holdings' idea concerning branding would help boost retail sales. All 16 interviewees gave this notion the thumbs down. As they pointed out, for the type of products that Callard supplied – generally gifts bought for their novelty and low price – consumers were not "brand conscious." Consequently, Callard Holdings didn't introduce the proposed branding policy. They saved a lot of money and misdirected effort by disregarding Pete's bias.

Instead, the company channeled its resources into responding to a surprise finding that came to light from the interviews. The retailers had reported being shunted around Callard Holdings whenever they made an enquiry or had a problem. This *did* affect retail sales because, in their frustration, the retailers leaned towards stocking competitors' products. Consequently, Callard allocated resources to implementing a new system to ensure that the appropriate staff took ownership of retailers' queries.

As we can see, instead of guessing at his customers' needs, Pete should have focused his attention on the key things only a CEO can do (see Exhibit 5.7).

Your Strategic Plan and Business Model

Writing the strategic plan for an organization or business unit is a monumental task. Think about it. It requires you to articulate the relationships your entity has with its key stakeholders – not just customers – and *design* these for the future.

Implementation is another important phase in the strategic planning process. Little wonder then that we have so much trouble achieving the desired result. Here are some suggestions:

Build Off Your Business Model. In the private sector, a business model describes how a firm generates revenue and makes a profit. In the not-for-profit sector, it's how an organization obtains funds and balances its books. In the public sector, it's how a government organization works within budget to deliver services effectively. Understanding this for your organization, whatever its type, is an essential first step to developing strategy and competitive advantage. In the case of Sunshine Living (Exhibit 3.2), its "future situation" defined its strategic plan's scope and outcomes. The strategies within its plan were focused on achieving this future.

Remember Level of Analysis. Recognize that the fundamental stumbling block in addressing strategy involves the level of analysis. Otherwise, your participants will emerge bruised and battered from strategy sessions because they become conceptual wars, although at the time it may look like a mere difference of opinion regarding future strategic direction.

Exhibit 5.7   What Only the Strategic Plan Can Do

The *Harvard Business Review* contained an excellent article called "What Only the CEO Can Do," written by A.G. Lafley, the CEO of Proctor & Gamble.[7] In it, Lafley described the special position that CEOs occupy. He combined his nine years' experience as the CEO of P&G with the final thoughts of the management scholar Peter Drucker, who died in November 2005. Addressing the question, "What is the work of the CEO?" Lafley pointed out that, in the end, the chief executive is held solely responsible for the company's performance and results. These are governed by the diverse and often competing demands of *stakeholders*.

Lafley describes how a CEO is responsible for linking the outside of an organization to the inside, which involves four fundamental tasks. What struck me was how Lafley's "four tasks" also defined the role of a *strategic* plan. In fact, the article could have been re-written with "strategic plan" substituted for "CEO" throughout and still have made complete sense. This set me thinking that a good strategic plan at a minimum summarizes the outcome of a CEO's reflections in these four areas, and defines what the CEO needs to focus on in driving an organization. A strategic plan *is* the CEO in plan form! Here are his four tasks:

- Defining the meaningful outside
- Deciding what business you are in
- Balancing present and future
- Shaping values and standards

Recognize Action. Keep foremost in your mind what action is. Properly drafted, it is what individuals in organizations do. Avoid writing action when you mean to write strategy.

Understand Strategy. Effectively designed, strategy is the position taken on a strategic factor. Being clear about the difference between strategy and action, and knowing how to write both, will assist your organization to soar. My suggested metaphor, the volume control, will boost your ability to develop precision in your positioning statements.

Resist the Gravitational Pull. Be comforted in the knowledge that we all struggle with strategy. The reason? We gravitate to action because this is the natural level for all of us as individuals. Action is what we *do*. Developing strategy requires a mind shift – from the individual to the organization. But it isn't easy. This is why I've found it necessary to design a method and a discipline to get you there.

Notes

1 Porter, M.E. 1980. *Competitive strategy*. New York: The Free Press; and Porter M.E. 1985. *Competitive advantage*. New York: The Free Press.
2 For a review of the literature that employs the "strategy concept," see Ronda-Pupo, G.A. & Guerras-Martin, L.A. 2012. Dynamics of the evolution of the strategy concept 1962–2008: A co-word analysis. *Strategic Management Journal*, 33: 162–188.
3 Greising, D. & Kirk, J. 2004. McDonald's finds missing ingredient. *Chicago Tribune*, June 27; Steffens, M. 2011. The trailblazer at the Golden Arches. *The Sydney Morning Herald Weekend Business*, March 5–6, p. 9.
4 Steffens, M. 2011. McDonald's looks at a diet Big Mac in health push. *The Sydney Morning Herald Weekend Business*, March 5–6, p. 3.
5 LaFrenz, C. 2008. Takeaways try to junk the junk food image. *The Weekend Australian Financial Review*, September 27–28, p. 12.
6 An observation also made by Richard Rumelt. See Rumelt, R.P. 2011. *Good strategy, bad strategy*. New York: Crown Business.
7 Lafley, A.G. 2009. What only the CEO can do. *Harvard Business Review*, May: 54–62.

Chapter 6

Stakeholder Perspective
Admit Stakeholders Know Strategies

Have you ever noticed how good we are at developing strategy? If by "we" you thought I meant "management," wrong. I mean you and I as customers. Think about it. As customers, you and I are continually designing strategies with queries that go like: "Why don't they..." "Wouldn't you think they'd..." Sometimes our suggestions are very specific. We go to a department store and on the strategic factor of product range, we have numerous suggestions as to what should be added or deleted. We also may have specific proposals on store presentation: the layout, lighting and color scheme, perhaps. And so it goes on, with airlines, telephone companies, banks – every organization, business and government department we deal with. We're continually designing strategies for them.

The fact that organizations have two quite different worlds – the outside and the inside – fascinates me. Yet the external world escapes many time-poor managers completely, even though it's right under their noses. My experience has been that most CEOs and their senior executive teams, either through hubris or lack of awareness, become so absorbed with the internal world of their organizations that they miss the *real* external world altogether.

How can you tap into your organization's external world and produce effective strategy?

Outside-In Thinking

As a new graduate, I thought that when I became a manager, I'd "know stuff." As we've seen, however, there are two types of stuff. One lot is internal to the organization and is concerned with its operations. The other is external and is concerned with customers, suppliers, etc.

Managers, I now know, watch the internal and often political world keenly and are on top of what goes on there. Their survival depends on it, and it's in their face – hard to ignore really. But, to put it bluntly, unless they make a great effort to find out, they know very little about the *experience* of

DOI: 10.4324/9781003394976-7

customers or the other stakeholders. Even as new recruits, managers can quickly get "out of touch." The reason: they are trapped inside their organizations, where the focus is on running the organization machine, attending meetings, providing verbal and written reports, watching expenses, supervising other people, etc. Who has the time to think strategically? It's all operations. Consequently, managers engage in inside-out thinking rather than outside-in thinking.[1] This then distorts the reality of their existence.

Managers engage in inside-out thinking rather than outside-in thinking. This then distorts the reality of their existence.

Contrast the external, lively, inventive, inquiring and downright disruptive world that you and I inhabit as customers with the internal world of the executive.

Michael Chaney of Wesfarmers, Australia's eighth largest company by market capitalization, gave an honest response to the question: "How much time do you spend focusing on strategy?" (He was CEO at the time):

> When I am in Perth, I spend around 85 per cent of my time in meetings, but they are meetings of a whole lot of sorts, ranging from board meetings to one-on-one, where someone might come in, for example, to talk about a personnel issue. As a result of that, the amount of time I spend thinking about strategy in the office is almost zero. The time I think more on strategy is if I wake up at 3am, or if I am on a plane, or down at our beach house, or in my workshop doing woodwork – the time when your mind is free of the day-to-day tasks, and you can start thinking about some different issues. That is why it is valuable doing other things.[2]

But time and work pressure are not the only impediments to keeping in touch with the outside world and developing successful strategy. Hubris and downright disdain can be major players.

Louis Gerstner was CEO and Chairman of IBM during its turnaround days. In the chapter "An Inside-Out World" from his book, *Who Says Elephants Can't Dance*, he had this to say regarding being cut off from reality and the customer experience:

> To someone arriving at IBM from the outside, there was a kind of hothouse quality to the place. It was like an isolated tropical ecosystem that had been cut off from the world for too long. As a result, it had spawned some fairly exotic life-forms that were to be found nowhere else. And because IBM was so deeply inbred and ingrown, so preoccupied with its own rules and conflicts, it had lost its robustness. It had become extremely vulnerable to attack from the outside.

This hermetically sealed quality – an institutional viewpoint that anything important started inside the company – was, I believe, the root cause of many of our problems. To appreciate how widespread the dysfunction was, I need to describe briefly some of its manifestations.

They included a general disinterest in customer needs, accompanied by a preoccupation with internal politics. There was general permission to stop projects dead in their tracks, a bureaucratic infrastructure that defended turf instead of promoting collaboration, and a management class that presided rather than acted. IBM even had a language all its own.[3]

This inwardly focused, cut-off world was also present at Proctor & Gamble (P&G) when A.G. Lafley took over as CEO during a crisis. As Lafley noted:

In China, for instance, we had no choice but to visit consumers where they lived and observe them where they shopped. Coming home to our global headquarters, in Cincinnati, I was struck as I walked the office halls by how many employees were glued to their computers and how much of each day people spent mired in internal meetings with other P&Gers. We were losing touch with consumers. We were not out in the competitive pressure cooker that is the marketplace. Too often we were working on initiatives consumers did not want and incurring costs that consumers should not have to pay for.[4]

Addressing Malfunction

The disconnected worlds of P&G and IBM are all too common; "being out of touch" becomes the norm. I see this across all industries, with the bright star in any of them being the organization that reverses the gravitational pull of its members focusing internally. But you need a method to do this. Otherwise, the consequence is inevitable: plodding performance at best.

"Being out of touch" becomes the norm.

Louis Gerstner, A.G. Lafley and other CEOs note the isolated and out-of-touch world that most executives live in. So, before we get to the ahead-of-the-curve world of Apple's Steve Jobs, we first have to climb out of the mire. Lafley saw the need for a cultural and mindset change at Proctor & Gamble. As he put it: "We won't succeed without a deep understanding of external stakeholders and their competing interests, and how those interests correspond with the capabilities and limitations of the organization."[5] This, of course, has been my message in this book. Keeping this approach paramount is the key to organizational success. Lafley acknowledges the struggle: "I give more attention to internal demands than I should; I constantly fight the gravitational pull from the inside."[6]

Other CEOs have expressed the importance of first-hand information in developing corporate strategy. The CEO of the electricity supplier Duke Energy in the US, James E. Rogers, speaks of his "100 days of listening" when he first took on the role: "The idea was to meet with the company's many stakeholders before taking action. That would help me to identify the issues, set priorities, figure out whom I could trust, and start repairing and rebuilding relationships."[7]

Kevin Peters, President for North America of Office Depot, an office products retailer with 22,500 staff, describes his approach in taking over as CEO. He visited 70 stores in 15 or more states in several weeks. He writes:

> During most of my visits, though, I managed to stay incognito, and I came away having learned a big lesson: Our mystery-shopping scores were correct. You know what was flawed? Our scoring system. We were asking the wrong questions. We were asking, Are the floors clean? Are the shelves full of inventory? Are the store windows clean? Have the bathrooms been cleaned recently?… My conversations with customers gave me three insights into how we should transform our business to become more competitive: One, we had to reduce the size of our stores. They were too large and too difficult to shop in. Two, we had to dramatically improve the in-store experience for our customers. That meant retraining our associates to stop focusing on the things our existing system had incentivized them to do and focus on customers instead. Three, we had to look beyond office products to provide other services our customers wanted. They wanted copying, printing, and shipping. They wanted help installing software and fixing computers. We needed to expand our offerings if we were to remain relevant to our customers.[8]

Peters would never have gained these insights if he had not started to ask the right questions (see Exhibit 6.1).

Stakeholder Experience

One step along the path from average to excellent is the adoption of the stakeholder framework outlined in the previous chapters of this book. Here I wish to go micro; that is, I want to look more deeply at what Steve Jobs described as the "customer experience." I want to take the concept of "experience" beyond customers to incorporate the stakeholders of all organization types, also encompassing the public and not-for-profit sectors, and include suppliers, donors, volunteers, shareholders, funding bodies, etc. Each group has its own "experience" of an organization, which differs from management.

Exhibit 6.1   Asking the Right Questions

Kenichi Ohmae, who used to head the McKinsey consulting firm in Japan, once consulted to Japanese firms that made coffee percolators. He examined this question: What makes a good coffee? and noted:

> Getting back to strategy means getting back to a deep understanding of what a product is about. Some time back, for example, a Japanese home appliance company was trying to develop a coffee percolator. Should it be a General Electric-type percolator, executives wondered? Should it be the same drip-type that Philips makes? Larger? Smaller? I urged them to ask a different kind of question: Why do people drink coffee? What are they looking for when they do? If your objective is to serve the customer better, then shouldn't you understand why that customer drinks coffee in the first place? Then you would know what kind of percolator to make.[9]

The answer to this fundamental question, they found, was "good taste." So, Kenichi Ohmae asked the company's technicians what they were doing to produce a good-tasting cup of coffee. Here's what he found:

> They said they were trying to design a good percolator. I asked them what influences the taste in a cup of coffee. No one knew. That became the next question we had to answer. It turns out that lots of things can affect taste – the beans, the temperature, the water. We did our homework and discovered all the things that affect taste... Of all the factors, water quality, we learned, made the greatest difference. The percolator in design at the time, however, didn't take water quality into account at all... We discovered next the grain distribution and the time between grinding the beans and pouring in the water were crucial. As a result we began to think about the product and its necessary features in a new way. It *had* to have a built-in dechlorinating function. It *had* to have a built-in grinder. All the customer should have to do is pour in water and beans.[10]

I want to take the concept of "experience" beyond customers to incorporate the stakeholders of all organization types, also encompassing the public and not-for-profit sectors, and include suppliers, donors, volunteers, shareholders, funding bodies, etc.

Let's look at this word "experience" in the case of a restaurant.

When you visit a restaurant, you approach it from the street. You notice how difficult or easy it is to park. You observe the mess, or not, on the footpath. You see the restaurant's logo and shop front. You get annoyed if the restaurant's door is difficult to open. You take note of the light level in the place – too dark, too bright. You pick up a bad vibe from the waiter. You observe the selections on the menu. All this, and you haven't even tasted the food yet! You'll make many observations during the evening, all part of your *experience*. You have fresh eyes. You're thinking is *outside-in*. (See Exhibit 6.2 for another example of "fresh eyes.")

Exhibit 6.2 Fresh Eyes – For Now

Mindy Grossman describes how when she became CEO of HSN (Home Shopping Network), she brought with her, what I would call, "fresh eyes." She describes her once-only, outside-in opportunity thus: "I'd never watched a home shopping channel… So, I started channel surfing. HSN wasn't easy to watch. It was very hard-sell. The aesthetics were dated. The products weren't aspirational and didn't seem very relevant. I could see from the numbers that HSN wasn't growing and was a very distant number two to QVC. At the time, I was an aficionado of Food Network and HGTV. So, I'd flip back and forth between HSN, QVC, HGTV, and Food Network, trying to get ideas. The only thing I liked on HSN was Wolfgang Puck selling cookware. He was funny and engaging. He gave you recipes. Even if you didn't want to buy anything, you could watch Wolfgang for an hour. And I had this "aha" moment: I realized that HSN really needed to become more of a lifestyle network that would inspire people through products."[11]

What does the restaurant owner do? She parks in a reserved parking space at the back of the restaurant. She enters the restaurant from the back door. On entering, as she is also the chef, she needs to make sure that the produce she has ordered has arrived, that preparations are underway for cooking and that she finds a replacement for the staff member who is sick.

That's her *experience*. Her eyes are stale. She's seen the restaurant all too often. She thinks about her business *inside-out*.

As I've noted previously, inside-out thinking is the inevitable consequence of becoming a member of an organization. As a customer, you see only too well what department stores, bookshops and airlines need to do to lift their game. And you'll tell any and everyone who cares to listen. But once you take that job at one of these places, you quickly lose that fresh outside-in view. You become like the restaurant owner. You think inside-out.

The good news is that once you accept that, as a member of an organization no matter your rank, you've got the blinkers on, and you've generated blind spots – you're free! Free to stop pretending that you know the ingredients of success for your business, free to say as a manager, "I don't know," and not feel incompetent, free to get out from behind your desk, or out of the kitchen, and talk to customers and other stakeholders and listen to their views.

I'm not suggesting here that the ideas you and I might generate for all the organizations we interact with come ready-made for execution. Some do, and some don't. Take, for example, a suggestion you might have on how airline staff could address passengers more politely. That suggestion can be implemented readily through improved staff selection procedures and training. But other ideas can be a long way off in terms of invention. Take, for instance, the mobile or cellular phone. The idea for that came from a customer saying: Wouldn't it be great if we could use a phone wherever we were? That same customer, of course, couldn't tell an organization how to do it. Complex engineering knowledge was required. But the *idea* came from a customer.

**Complex engineering knowledge was required. But the *idea*
came from a customer**.

How do you tap into this world?

Since we acknowledge that as captives in their own organizations, managers, R&D staff, and marketing professionals have great trouble getting into customers' shoes, why not elicit the help of others closer to the customer? The consumer-products giant Proctor & Gamble (P&G) did just that in recognizing that important innovation was increasingly being conducted at small entrepreneurial companies. As two senior executives in innovation and R&D at P&G point out:

> Most companies are still clinging to what we call the invention model, centered on a bricks-and-mortar R&D infrastructure and the idea that their innovation must principally reside within their own four walls.

To be sure, these companies are increasingly trying to buttress their laboring R&D departments with acquisitions, alliances, licensing, and selective innovation outsourcing. And they're launching Skunk Works [a largely autonomous group working on a secret project], improving collaboration between marketing and R&D, tightening go-to-market criteria, and strengthening product portfolio management. But these are incremental changes, bandages on a broken model.[12]

Instead, P&G created the "connect and develop" innovation model that enabled it to link to a vast network of outside innovators and thus identify promising solutions around the globe.

Ethnography is the classification of human cultural and racial groups. It involves Western anthropologists visiting exotic locations and trying to understand social and cultural dynamics. Researchers immerse themselves in the communities they study and basically "hang out" with the locals. This approach is being increasingly applied in business and especially to understanding customers and their needs, as well as their usage of products and services. It entails listening to customers' stories.

Harley-Davidson has employed this technique in motorbikes, P&G and SC Johnson in fast-moving consumer goods, and Microsoft and Intel in technology. The basic difference between an ethnographic approach and traditional market research is that the latter often leads respondents down a particular line of inquiry constructed by the researchers beforehand.

As consultant Charlie Cochrane puts it: "With ethnography, you try to get people to tell their own stories around the subject area and, in that process, the insights become framed around whatever meaning is relevant to the participants rather than a construct that you as the researcher is imposing." With conventional qualitative research, he continues: "You can cover off an extensive agenda in a short timeframe if you ask pointed questions. But what you don't always get from that are the revelations that ethnography can deliver. That is when people talk about something in a new and different way, which can lead to a whole different slant on the problem."[13] (See Exhibit 6.3 on Steve Jobs' story.)

Getting Into the Skin of Your Stakeholders

Here are a few suggestions for achieving the stakeholder experience in your organization:

Humility. You may have noticed that effective CEOs and managers have this quality. They listen. They observe. They learn. Then they translate this knowledge into reality for their organizations. This is what true leadership is. It's not a know-it-all approach. Hubris has no place in outside-in

---

Exhibit 6.3   Steve Jobs and the Customer Experience

Steve Jobs never lost the "touch," working hard over his period as CEO of Apple to remain involved with the "customer experience." Apple's early beginnings illustrate the advantage of having a CEO who is in touch with what customers really want. In 1979, when Apple Computers was just two years old, Jobs visited the Xerox research center. The giant Xerox was thinking of buying into Apple at that time and allowed Jobs to go on a tour. The visit revealed a personal computer, the Alto, which had a "mouse," a feature then unknown to all but a few. The mouse opened and closed another innovation, "windows" on the computer screen. Malcolm Gladwell, who captured this incident, writes: "[Jobs] raced back to Apple and demanded that the team... change course. He wanted menus on the screen. He wanted windows. He wanted a mouse. The result was the Macintosh, perhaps the most famous product in the history of Silicon Valley. 'If Xerox had known what it had and had taken advantage of its real opportunities,' Jobs said, years later, 'it could have been as big as IBM plus Microsoft plus Xerox combined – and the largest high-technology company in the world.'"[14] Instead, Xerox had little commercial success with its Alto and departed the field of personal computers.

---

thinking and effective strategy. Fear is also an enemy. Many managers are afraid to admit, "I don't know," when it comes to developing a strategy to make an organization successful. Understanding stakeholders is coupled with a listen-and-learn attitude, not a tell-them one.

Organization Systems. If your company's two-day planning workshop involves a group of senior executives getting together to develop your strategic plan, and they do so there and then, my guess is it's not a *strategic* plan at all. The organization is looking inside-out and, I suggest, it doesn't have all the answers. I'd go further. It probably hasn't even asked the right questions (see Exhibit 6.1). A strategic plan must be developed via outside-in thinking. But this is only one example of an organizational process that is poorly conceived. Outside-in thinking impacts product and service design methods, ideas for attracting and retaining staff, gaining the support of corporate sponsors and so on.

Tapping Into Stakeholders. My example earlier of visiting a restaurant illustrates clearly outside-in thinking vs. inside-out thinking. You, or a third party you may commission, can start obtaining the outside-in view of your business through interviews. But the design of the interview must allow the interviewee to go on the "customer (or other stakeholder) journey." You want, for example, to hear how the customer made the decision to buy from you or the competition. If employees are the focus, you may want to know clearly how "image" is defined by a prospective employee. On the criteria that emerge from the stories, you also want to know how your organization performed and whether there are any suggestions that will improve performance – and hence competitiveness. It's important, though, to make the session about *story-listening*. You need to listen to the customer's story in detail and, if possible, record it for later analysis. It's also important that any interview takes place soon after the customer's shopping trip or the experience of another stakeholder. Leave it too long, and people forget the detail; they are left with only vague impressions.

Actual and Potential. Any interviews should be with your current customers and other stakeholders, of course. But they should take place with your *potential* customers and stakeholders as well. Customers come in two types: those currently buying from your competitors and the "non-customers." Non-customers are individuals or companies that don't use your products or services or your competitors' products or services at all. The Australian wine company, Yellowtail, is credited with not only switching US wine drinkers to their brand but, through their simple packaging, plain labeling and low pricing, converting US non-wine drinkers into wine drinkers.[15] Your interviews should include "current" and "potential" categories for your stakeholders if you intend to truly tap into ideas for the long term.

Listen and Succeed. Kevin Costner famously uttered the line "if you build it, they will come" in the film *Field of Dreams*, a personal favorite of mine. Costner had faith that if he flattened part of his cornfield and built a baseball diamond in it, all the baseball legends from previous eras would turn up. And, despite all the doubters, they did. In other words, if you provide what people want, they will make the journey to join you; the trick is in being sure you know what people want. And to know that, you need to listen to them. Over the years, based on my experience as a manager and consultant and as an observer of managers making decisions, I've discovered that effective CEOs and managers are good listeners. But they're more than that. They know *who* to listen to, and in listening to the right people, they become outside-in thinkers. If you listen, you will succeed.

Notes

1 I first went to print with "outside-in thinking" in 2001 in my book *Strategic factors: Develop and measure winning strategy*. Sydney: President Press. This was republished in 2005 by Elsevier Butterworth-Heimemann as *Strategic planning*

and performance management. Barbara Bund published a book in 2006, which I only discovered in mid-2011, called *The outside-in corporation.* New York: McGraw-Hill.

2 Stinton, D. 2003. Michael Chaney, *Scoop*, Autumn: 38–41.

3 Gerstner, L.V. 2002. *Who says elephants can't dance?* New York: Harper Business, p. 189.

4 Lafley, A.G. 2009. What only the CEO can do, *Harvard Business Review*, May: 54–62, p. 57.

5 Ibid., p. 56.

6 Ibid., p. 62.

7 Rogers, J.E. 2011. The CEO of Duke Energy on learning to work with green activists. *Harvard Business Review*, May: 51–54.

8 Peters, K. 2011. Office Depot's President on how "mystery shopping" helped spark a turnaround. *Harvard Business Review*, November: 47–50.

9 Ohmae, K. 1988. Getting back to strategy. *Harvard Business Review*, November–December: 149–156.

10 Ohmae, K. 1988. Getting back to strategy. *Harvard Business Review*, November–December: 149–156.

11 Grossman, M. 2011. HSN's CEO on fixing the shopping network's culture. *Harvard Business Review*, December, p. 44.

12 Huston, L. & Sakkab, N. 2006. Connect and develop: Inside Proctor & Gamble's new model for innovation. *Harvard Business Review*, March: 58–66.

13 The rise of ethnography: How market research has gone gonzo, *Knowledge@ Australian School of Business*, 2011, October 25.

14 Gladwell, M. 2011. Creation myth. *The New Yorker*, May 16.

15 Kim, W.C. & Mauborgne, R. 2005. *Blue ocean strategy.* Boston: Harvard Business School Press.

Chapter 7

Implementation

Disclose Implementation's Components

A few years ago, I was conducting a strategic planning seminar at one of the Hilton Hotels, and everything was going fine. Working through my agenda, I stressed the importance of *implementation*. "Think implementation first, not last." I repeated: "Implementation should not be an afterthought but your first thought."

I continued in this vein, emphasizing the importance of knowing how strategic plans would be used, reviewed and updated. "If you haven't worked out how you intend to use your plan, don't start planning until you do." I added that in figuring out how to translate the plan into action, they would be better equipped to design the structure and content of the strategic plan itself.

Implementation should not be an afterthought but your first thought.

During the coffee break, we all huddled around coffee, tea and croissants and chatted about the morning's proceedings. Terry, whose job was to develop an annual strategic plan for his large, not-for-profit organization, referred to my point by repeating it: "If you haven't worked out how you intend to use your plan, then don't start planning until you do." With a grin, he commented, "I don't want to go there – I mightn't have a job!" His experience was that his organization would develop a strategic plan year after year, although little of it would ever be implemented. Yet this didn't stop management from wading in each year and doing it again – without ever asking, "Why?"

It's generally acknowledged that organizations have a poor record when it comes to implementing their strategic plans. Terry knows that is true of his organization, but he's powerless to change it. So, he continues to go through an annual strategic planning process with low expectations of ever changing anything. You may be with Terry in this predicament.

DOI: 10.4324/9781003394976-8

It's generally acknowledged that organizations have a poor record when it comes to implementing their strategic plans.

It brings us back to a basic question. Wouldn't it be great if success could be reduced to a couple of basic dimensions? Life would certainly be simpler.

Take success in sport, for example, and swimming as a specific case. Individuals become champions when they know how to swim really well – right technique, right training – but also put that knowledge into practice. They've trained to the point where the winning technique becomes natural. They dive into that pool and leave the competition for dead. Staying with sport, how often have we seen the promising youngster who didn't obtain the right exposure to coaching fail to go on to champion status? Or in any sport, how often have we seen the individual who obtains all the privileges in coaching but who doesn't put in the required 10,000 hours to get to the top?[1]

Can we think of organizations in the same vein? I think we can.

Strategy and Execution

The success of any organization can be explained by two strategy fundamentals, the first of which is *formulation*: how an organization's or business unit's strategies are put together. Criteria here include:

- Do they focus on key stakeholders?
- Do they address positions on strategic factors?
- Are these positions likely to deliver a competitive advantage and achieve their stated objectives?

The second fundamental is *implementation*: ensuring that positions on strategic factors occur.[2]

Putting these two dimensions together produces the graph in Exhibit 7.1. You can plot your own organization on that graph – good or poor at formulation? Good or poor at implementation?

Overall, hardly any research data exists on poor implementation, although there is much anecdotal evidence from managers. I found a rare success estimate in a study by Walter Kiechel. He interviewed most of the major consulting firms, including BCG, Bain, McKinsey, Arthur D. Little and Strategic Planning Associates. He obtained an estimate of how many of the corporations they dealt with effectively implemented their strategies. The overall response? Less than 10 per cent.[3] It does not say that less than 10 per cent of *strategies* are implemented successfully – which is how Kiechel's result was reported by Henry Mintzberg.[4] It says that less than

Exhibit 7.1   Champions and Plodders

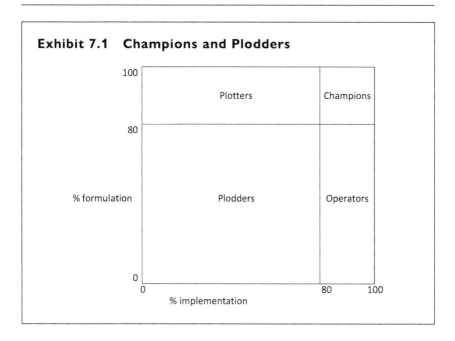

10 per cent of the *organizations* they worked with implemented their strategies effectively!

Kiechel's research is a rough estimate and was reported some time ago, in 1984. There's been a dearth of quantified data on this topic since. To help fill this gap, I undertook some initial research, investigating the extent to which strategic plans were *implemented* within the *planned period*, e.g., two years.

At the conclusion of two sets of seminars, I asked participants to respond to a questionnaire. Many delegates could not respond at all, either because they did not have the information required by the questionnaire or because their organization lacked a strategic plan altogether. A *written* strategic plan was needed to make the assessments called for. Following this, I studied 33 organizations in-depth, 29 of which were headquartered in Australia and New Zealand and four subsidiaries of foreign companies. This became The Competitive Potential Project. I gave it that name because, although all organizations have huge potential to succeed, few achieve that potential for the two basic reasons I've advanced: strategy and execution.

The sampled organizations came from a wide range of industries and varied in size from five to 15,000 employees, with a median size (middle value from highest to lowest) of 120. My consulting practice and seminar research confirmed that the *experiences* of these 33 entities in strategic planning were representative of the general population of organizations.

Respondents from the organizations were interviewed to check the initial questionnaire results, gather further information and understand the context. On the question of implementation, I investigated the percentage of *strategies* that were implemented during the expected period.

I found from my sample of 33 organizations that the median score on the percentage of implemented strategies during the specified period was 50.

So, what do we make of this figure? Only half of the strategies in strategic plans are implemented!

Based on my experience and anecdotal evidence, I feel that this result is certainly not underestimated. Due to work overload and lack of follow-up effort, I see many organizations develop their strategic plans only to have them sit on shelves gathering dust. I see other plans that, because of their structure and contents, are simply too vague and general to be executed. By contrast, I've witnessed very programmed approaches to implementing strategic plans. Even in these cases, achieving 100 per cent is highly problematic. So, overall, I am quite confident that 50 per cent is *not* an underestimate. But clearly, more research is required on this topic.

The labels in Exhibit 7.1 have come about by dividing the 33 organizations in my sample according to how well they did on formulation and implementation. I've constructed four quadrants: champions (good formulators/good implementers), plotters (good formulators/poor implementers), operators (poor formulators/good implementers) and plodders (poor formulators/poor implementers). I've set the cut-off point for champions on both scales at 80 per cent. I chose this number because, based on my examination of the cases and my observation in practice, I figured that any organization that could *implement* 80 per cent or more of its strategies, with 80 per cent or more of these being so well formulated as to be truly *competitive*, was doing quite well – a champion. (Ideally, of course, the figures should be 100 and 100, but we don't live in a perfect and unchanging world.)

Out of the 33 organizations examined, we got one champion, one plotter, five operators and *26 plodders*! Let's now turn to specifics. What is it that successful implementers do?

Make Strategy Happen via *Actions*

My experience over many years suggests that there are three specific elements to successful strategy execution. They can be summed up with the acronym *AMM – action, monitor and measure.*

As you now appreciate, a strategy is a position taken on a strategic factor, such as product range, designed to achieve competitive advantage. The essential feature of strategy, as we have already seen, is that it involves a position *of the organization* on that factor, e.g., broadening the product range to include fresh fruit and vegetables in addition to groceries.

Strategy is *not* action. *Action is what an individual does*. And it's action that moves strategy from desire to reality. Effective implementers design those actions clearly and precisely. Poor implementers leave this how-to-achieve step up in the air, loosely specified and poorly understood by those responsible for the strategy's execution. On the surface, writing action statements may seem easy. But there are many ways to stumble and fall – see Exhibit 7.2.

Strategy is *not* action. *Action is what an individual does*.

Exhibit 7.2   What a Group of Senior Managers Called "Actions"

A group of senior managers, left to their own devices, developed a list of actions to implement their strategies. Here's a sample from that list, with my comments. There are certainly many pitfalls along the way to developing effective actions.

"Action"	My Comment
"Streamlining policies and procedures"	Action-type words that end in "ing" are activities, not actions. Even if we convert this to "streamline policies and procedures" it's too vague to give to someone for completion by a certain date.
"Broaden online training"	Looks like an action, but it's not specific enough to give to someone to complete.
"Access external learning and development programs as required"	Again, it's non-specific, and "as required" suggests it's not the appropriate form of high-level action needed in a strategic plan.
"To develop a policy for an employee assistance program"	Actions don't start with "to" – objectives do.
"Research the market for an effective rewards and recognition program and prepare a report for senior management"	The action is clear, can be given to someone to undertake and can be assigned a completion date. It is the type of high-level action required in a strategic plan.

On the plus side, managers are generally more comfortable with action than strategy. Here are some guidelines.

Actions start with a verb, i.e., *undertake* research. The other essential element of an action is that it can be assigned to someone for execution – it's *doable*. It also has a *completion date*; it is not ongoing. Thus, "undertake research to assess what customers think of the company's service" is an action because it can be assigned to the Market Research Manager for completion by a certain date.

Why do managers often write *descriptions of activity* when they intend to set down actions? Take, for example, the statement "improve the quality of communications across the business." It starts with a verb, but it is too vague to be assigned to anyone or completed by a certain date. This distinction is crucial in separating actions from all those other statements that float around in strategy sessions. Over the years, I've found managers wrongly believing that if they cobble together a pile of *activities*, write the organization's vision statement and throw in a few financials, they've got a strategic plan! They haven't.

Leonards Construction illustrates the relationship between strategy and action as well as the way to write effective actions. Leonards is a successful medium-sized company that could have up to $400 million worth of projects on its books at any time. It employs 250 staff and engages a myriad of subcontractors. The company comprises three divisions: Construction, with 175 employees; Workshop, with 36 employees; and Facilities Management and Maintenance, with 14 employees. There are several people in head office with functions such as Finance and Administration.

Leonards Construction operates mainly in the state in which it has its headquarters, but it does have projects in other states. It undertakes the construction of factories, offices, schools, libraries, university buildings, hotels and the like. The company also contracts to do the internal fit-outs of existing buildings and has recently branched out to undertake facilities management: maintenance of office buildings, retail shopping centers and so on.

The purpose of the strategic planning and performance measurement project was to help grow the company significantly over the next five to ten years. As the CEO put it, the company needed to "ramp up its performance" and significantly change its results.

At one of our early meetings, I emphasized the importance of *implementation*. So, my proposal to assist them included developing an action plan, as an integral component of their strategic plan.

As a step to developing an effective strategic plan and a linked scorecard of key performance indicators, Leonards Construction's management team identified the company's key stakeholders:

- Construction Clients (customers who require buildings or related civil engineering work)
- Workshop Clients (customers who require joinery and the fit-out of buildings)
- Facilities Management Clients (property owners who require a service to manage and maintain their properties)
- Subcontractors (companies that provide labor and materials on contract to Leonards)
- Consultants (design professionals who provide consulting services either to the client or directly to Leonards)
- Materials Suppliers (companies that provide materials, plant and equipment to Leonards)
- Staff (personnel employed directly by Leonards)
- Shareholders (the owners of the company)

Notice how clients have been segmented into three groups, coinciding with the three divisions within the company, although this internal structure wasn't the reason for the split in the client base. Rather, it was vice versa.

The CEO undertook a task that was not only instrumental in getting additional ideas for the Strategy Workshop that was to follow but was also fundamental to obtaining buy-in by all staff to the planning process and later-stage *implementation*. What he did was ask *all* employees, via the company's email system, to submit *any* ideas, suggestions, etc., that they would like the strategy team to consider during the forthcoming Strategy Workshop. These were collected via a "discussion forum" on the company's intranet, which allowed *every* employee to see every other employee's contribution on a page and add to it if they wished.

Over the following weeks, the contributions and suggestions flowed in. As promised, everyone was considered by the management team at the two-day Strategy Workshop. Exhibit 7.3 shows the actions that appeared in Leonards Construction's strategic plan for Workshop Clients.

Exhibit 7.3   Actions Implement Strategy

Strategy	Action	Responsibility	Completion Date
Position on *product quality*: A level that places the company at the top end of industry standards	Establish better relationships with timber suppliers and acquaint them with our quality standards as they apply to supplies	Purchasing Officer	25 March 20XX
	Identify the Workshop Division's capability gap and train all workshop employees in quality management	Quality Supervisor	30 April 20XX
	Install a more effective inspection system for finished products before their shipping to customers	Workshop Manager	30 June 20XX
Position on *customer service*: Includes extensive technical advice on using our products in addition to our regular service	Design an internal system for channeling technical inquiries to the appropriately qualified staff	Office Manager	24 May 20XX
	Notify current and potential customers of the availability of the additional technical advice	Sales Manager	30 July 20XX

Strategy	Action	Responsibility	Completion Date
Position on *lead times*: Tailored for individual client orders to a period commensurate with individual clients' construction constraints	Set up a schedule to make components that are standard for stock rather than to order	Production Supervisor	25 April 20XX
	Institute a system that allows for greater flexibility in working hours to cope with peak-and-trough demands for products	Workshop Manager	30 May 20XX
	Organize "partner" relationships with a select group of suppliers so they can respond more effectively to shortened lead times	Purchasing Officer	14 June 20XX
Position on *location*: Incorporate agencies in other states, but outside the capital cities in those states, to expand the company's reach	Research likely agencies in major centers outside the capital cities and develop draft agency agreement in preparation for proposed expansion	Sales Manager	31 August 20XX

Monitoring Is Essential

Even if you have the actions in place that are necessary to implement your organization's strategies, you must monitor their execution. Failure to do so has affected politicians as well as CEOs.

Nick Greiner was once Premier of the State of New South Wales in Australia. He reflected on his years as Premier and his success, or lack of it, in that role. Regarding monitoring, he had this to say; "I think a lot of leaders still are insufficiently concerned about the execution, the completion of the strategy rather than simply determining that it's right."[5] Greiner is now a full-time, and very busy, director of major companies. He was addressing a gathering of company directors at the time of his remarks and clearly gave his fellow directors an important message: Monitoring is extremely important. Don't overlook it!

Monitoring is extremely important. Don't overlook it!

Here I'd like to take a close look at the *monitoring practices* of some of the 33 cases from The Competitive Potential Project. APA (all names are fictitious) is one of the six effective implementers from my sample and was classified as an "operator." This government-owned business covers the national population under an accident insurance scheme. It also spends a significant proportion of its resources on measuring performance and monitoring and reporting progress against plans. I did a count. It has 2,000 employees, four "accountability documents" (such as a business plan, a service agreement for government, and a statement of intent for its board of directors), four "goals" (such as injury prevention), eight "key deliverables" (such as claimants' satisfaction), 40 "KPIs" (key performance indicators), 60 "supporting measures," an 80-page quarterly report to the government Minister in charge, a 30-page "summary" of that report for management and a four-page monthly summary on 12 of the KPIs for its board. The result is a reported 80 per cent achievement on implementation – but clearly through much hard work!

This hard work is evident in the five other organizations that did well on implementation in my research. Many have some of APA's monitoring mechanisms in place. One is Bullock, our one "champion," a 300-employee unit in business publishing. It reportedly scored 100 per cent for implementation. Bullock spent a considerable amount of time and effort on monitoring, with computerized reports, regular meetings and personal follow-ups. Overall, there was great attention to detail and a high level of thoroughness – creating the same impression you get when visiting a world-class manufacturing business like Toyota.[6]

Another effective implementer is Xtreme, an "operator" and a not-for-profit 700-employee ambulance service. As an ambulance service, it supplies emergency transport for patients involved in accidents and other incidents. Half of its funds come from the government, while the remainder comes from subscribers and users. Xtreme is strongly influenced by the nature of its industry: patient pick-ups and deliveries, emergencies, risk and peoples' lives. As a result, monitoring is paramount and execution essential.

I suggest to all clients that their senior management team visit their strategic plan each month. I propose making "Progress on the Strategic Plan" the first item on their agenda. This keeps the plan in focus and makes it a driver of managers' actions – and business performance. Management teams agree that is a good idea, which means that each month their plan will be reviewed and updated, with *new actions added as needed*. The latter will be determined by whether conditions in the industry or planning assumptions have altered and, consequently, strategies. Thus, the organization's plan will never be out-of-date but always fresh and current. The management team and other staff will keep their focus on it, and it will have a major impact on decision-making. Each manager whose actions are to be completed around the time of the meeting will report results or progress.

I suggest to all clients that their senior management team visit their strategic plan each month.

Driving It Home Through *Measures*

Now we come to the second M in my AMM (action, monitor and measure) acronym. And measurement is terribly important to successful implementation. My approach involves a Focused Scorecard – note the term "focused," not "balanced."[7] This involves a set of measures clustered around an organization's *key* stakeholders. (In the Balanced Scorecard, the measures fall into four pre-set categories.)

Let's look at one CEO's approach to linking his organization's strategic plan to a scorecard of key performance indicators.

Restart was established in response to the inability of existing educational and treatment facilities to either accept autism or address the specific needs of children and adults with autism, as well as their families. Since its inception, the organization has developed and provided desperately needed services and programs for many thousands of children, adolescents and young adults with autism. Today, Restart is the leading service provider for all autism spectrum disorders. It offers:

- Direct services for children in the form of early intervention and schooling, incorporating specialty schools, satellite classes, education and family support, assessment, transition and itinerant education support.
- Direct services for adults in the form of employment, training and accommodation.

- Advice and assistance for those many families who receive inadequate or inappropriate services or for whom there are no services at all.
- A central resource for families and services seeking information and advice about autism spectrum disorders.
- Below is an extract from my interview with Peter, Restart's CEO.

Graham: Let's start with actions. What's the link between actions and strategies in your organization?

Peter: One of the important things we've done is to use your system for our corporate strategic plan and the scorecard for the organization. Our strategic plan for the organization drops down to an action plan for each business unit.

G: And I noted that the actions link back to your strategies.

P: Exactly. So, the action plan is the plan for the coming year based on our rolling three-year strategic plan.

G: And how do you sustain momentum in implementing your strategic plan?

P: Our process is rigorous. I meet with every member of the Executive monthly, and we look at the strategic plan and review where we're going. It seems to have worked much better in our organization to have this regular ongoing, but incredibly thorough, process.

G: I notice from your scorecard [Exhibit 7.4] that you focus on stakeholders. Any comments on that?

P: We've been incredibly focused on our *key stakeholders*. That focus has been the driver of where we wanted to go. The clarity that the plan has brought has meant that we've become, I think, a highly successful organization. When I joined, we had a turnover of $33 million, and in the current year, we have a turnover of $280 million. That's pretty satisfactory, that point of growth. Again, when I started, we could only count that we were helping 3,000 people. In the current year, we're helping more than 30,000. We can identify and count them. The stakeholder focus is absolutely spot on.

G: And when do you report progress on your plan and scorecard?

P: It's reported on at every monthly board meeting, monthly executive meeting and at managers' meetings. So, people are up to date with where they are for the whole organization.

G: Is it working well?

P: Absolutely. In fact, that's why nine years ago I rocked along to your seminar. The board was saying that the previous CEO had no measurables. She was all words. It's been one of the toughest things to do, to try and get measurables. But we have some now and they have been very useful indicators. They have pushed us to gradually get a more robust organization. So yes, I'm a strong believer in measurables.

G: You mentioned that over the years you've been able to reduce the number of measures in your scorecard. How have you been able to do this and why?

P: In the coming year we'll have 16 KPIs for the organization. We've done it really through experience and by focusing on those few measures that are central to implementing our strategies and achieving the organization's objectives.

Exhibit 7.4   Restart's Focused Scorecard

Key Stakeholder	Key Performance Indicator
People with Disorder & Their Families	# people with disorder in contact with Restart # service locations # service partners (includes government and non-government providers) # students who transition from Restart's schools # school places
Governments	$m received from governments (including capital)
Donors & Supporters	$m net received from fundraising (including capital donations) # donors
Staff	% voluntary employee turnover (including contract staff) # lost time injury frequency rate

Members	$m surplus in operating budget
	$m in strategic investment portfolio
	$ cash at period end
	$ funding capacity
	# media stories involving Restart and/or its services
	# current research, evaluation and continuous improvement projects

---

Boosting Your Implementation Success

Implementation Can Be the Difference. In his splendid book *Who Says Elephants Can't Dance?*[8] Louis Gerstner, CEO of IBM during its major turnaround, describes the levers he had to pull to produce this result. He makes the interesting and important point that in some industries, companies develop similar strategies, but what distinguishes those that succeed from those that don't is not necessarily the strategies themselves; it is their *execution* – his word. As Gerstner puts it: "All of the great companies in the world out-execute their competitors day in and day out in the marketplace, in their manufacturing plants, in their logistics, in their inventory turns – in just about everything they do. Rarely do great companies have a proprietary position that insulates them from the constant hand-to-hand combat of competition."[9]

Design Real Actions. It's an old saying: actions speak louder than words. We talk a lot about what we're going to do but often never get around to doing it. In strategic plans, words do come cheap. Your organization will have to struggle to go beyond words to action. But here's the rub: it's strategy that gives action meaning. Without strategy it is just meaningless activity. *Action needs strategy for meaning; strategy needs action for execution.* And action is what individuals do – but make sure they're real actions.

Action needs strategy for meaning; strategy needs action for execution.

Keep Watch. AMM stands for action, *monitor* and measure. Actions, properly drafted, are essential to implementing your strategy. But the successful completion of those actions depends on your overseeing them, along with those responsible for carrying them out. Be aware that one of the major causes of poor implementation is organization structure, i.e., how people at the different levels of your organization communicate and interact. The common view is that strategy is decided at the top but implemented at the bottom. In this handover of responsibility, it's not unusual for the ball to be dropped when senior management moves on to its next "big thing." As a result, out goes an unintended signal: "Implementation is tedious and not that important."[10] This is precisely the wrong signal if your organization wants to achieve real success from the positions designed in its strategies.

When your senior management appears to lose interest, lower-level managers, already overloaded, note the attitude and think, "What the hell – I'm too busy, anyway. Besides, they're going to come up with some other big idea soon, which we'll play with for a while and drop. They'll forget." And this is often exactly what happens. Because of a lack of monitoring, poor strategy execution becomes taken for granted.

Because of a lack of monitoring, poor strategy execution becomes taken for granted.

Measure Around Stakeholders. I'm a strong advocate for developing performance measures around key stakeholders.[11] My experience has been that this procedure leads CEOs and their executive teams to think through their organization's relationships with the outside world and address the question of "success" thoroughly. This stakeholder approach to measurement fits hand-in-glove with the previously outlined method for developing your organization's strategies. I don't advocate that you follow an off-the-shelf solution such as the Balanced Scorecard – apart from any theoretical reasons, you'd now have your strategies and measures developed on two quite different platforms!

Design Your Plan's Structure. Lastly, be alert to the fact that a major cause of poor implementation of strategic plans lies in the plans themselves. Their structure and content may make them impossible to implement. Your current strategic plan may actually be a vague document that qualifies as a "wish list." With such a document, how can you develop a series of programmed actions and detailed measures to drive the execution of your strategies?

Notes

1 Malcolm Gladwell writes about "the 10,000-hour rule" in Gladwell, M. 2008. *Outliers*. London: Penguin Books.

2 In his study, William Egelhoff described these two dimensions as "competitive styles" and focused on US and Japanese semiconductor producers. See Egelhoff, W.G. 1993. Good strategy or great strategy implementation – two ways of competing in global markets. *Sloan Management Review*, Winter: 37–50.

3 Kiechel, W. 1984. Sniping at strategic planning. *Planning Review*, May: 8–11.

4 Mintzberg, H. 1994. *The rise and fall of strategic planning*. Hemel Hempstead: Prentice Hall, p. 25.

5 Leadership: heroic or humble, go your own way. *NSW Director*, Winter 2010.

6 This jaw-dropping attention to detail has been witnessed by the author. It is also documented in Spear, S. & Bowen, H.K. 1999. Decoding the DNA of the Toyota production system. *Harvard Business Review*, September–October: 96–106. See also Osono, E., Shimizu, N. & Takeuchi, H. 2008. *Extreme Toyota*. Hoboken: Wiley.

7 My views on the shortcomings of the 'balanced scorecard' and the strength of a stakeholder approach can be found in Kenny, G. 2003. Balanced scorecard: Why it isn't working. *Management*, March: 32–34; Kenny, G. 2010. Ditching the balanced scorecard. *National Accountant*, December–January: 22–24.

8 Gerstner, L. 2002. *Who says elephants can't dance?* New York: Harper Business.

9 Ibid., p. 230.

10 Lawrence Hrebiniak refers unflatteringly to the "grunts" handling execution while top-level managers do the planning. See Hrebiniak, L.G. 2005. *Making strategy work*. Upper Saddle River: Wharton School Publishing, p. 7.

11 Kenny, G. 2001. *Strategic factors: Develop and measure winning strategy*. Sydney: President Press. Re-published in 2005 by Elsevier Butterworth-Heinemann as *Strategic planning and performance management*.

Chapter 8

Strategy Pitfalls
Unveil Strategy's Inner Logic

One February morning, I found myself at breakfast in the restaurant of my hotel in Port Moresby, Papua New Guinea. I was there to assist a client in strategic planning and performance measurement. I casually opened the newspaper that was nearby, *The Business Times*. Outlined over several pages was the *Corporate Plan* of the Department of Treasury of the Papua New Guinea Government. It was published in full. I must admit I was shocked. Not that the Treasury had made their plan public, but that they had spent the money for so much newspaper space to tell people about it. Was the public really so interested? I wondered.

I then started taking in the document's details. I found myself in critical mode and looking for certain features in the plan. I reviewed the relationship of the parts to each other, on the lookout for any inconsistencies, any gaps in the material. I was watchful for repetition. In short, I was testing the plan's *inner logic*.

The PNG plan did have its flaws. It developed, for example, its key strategies according to key performance areas: Policy, Governance, Budget and Operations. With this structure, the "strategies" turned out to be actions. There was no *strategic* perspective there; probably just business as usual.

But, as I've found, this strategic plan wasn't alone when it comes to faulty structure driving poor content.

As another example, take any book with a title like *How to Write a Successful Business Plan*. Though talking competitiveness, it will walk operations. The standard plan structure, based on *business functions* such as Marketing, Accounting and Operations, is devoid of key stakeholders and a strategic perspective. One such plan is divided into: "Executive Summary; Product/Service and Market Analysis; Marketing Plan; Operating Plan; Management and Personnel Plan; Legal Matters; Finance Plan; Action Plan."

Faulty structures truly abound. Take the mining company that organized its "strategies" according to "key issues" such as "Future Revenue Growth,"

DOI: 10.4324/9781003394976-9

"Contractor Availability," "Staff Skill Shortage," and so on. Then there's the private hospital that structured its plan and "strategies" around "critical success factors" that included "Capital Development," "Responsible Financial Management" and "Developing Key Partnerships," among others. Or the electricity-generating company that listed its "strategies" by "key result area," which included "Resource Management," "Environmental Responsibility" and "People."

All of these plan structures start and finish in a comfortable place: what management knows and does. They're developed by management teams and/or boards sitting in a room and depositing their inside-out perspectives into their "strategic plans." Little wonder such documents become business-as-usual and all-too-comfortable "strategic plans" that lack actual strategy.

I've developed an eight-part Inner Logic Checklist that you might employ (see Exhibit 8.1.). By using it, your management team and board of directors will be able to assess the soundness of any strategic plan you produce and thereby lift the effectiveness of your organization.

Exhibit 8.1 Inner Logic Checklist

1	Make sure your strategic plan follows a key stakeholder structure.
2	Make sure the key stakeholder structure you have identified isn't violated during the process of developing the strategies in your plan.
3	Make sure the organization objectives in your strategic plan are based on your key stakeholders and are consistent and measurable.
4	Make sure the measures developed for an objective actually relate to that objective and cover it comprehensively.
5	Make sure the strategic factors you have identified for your key stakeholders are from their perspective, outside-in.
6	Make sure the definitions of strategic factors are those of key stakeholders, not those of management.
7	Make sure your strategies aren't actions or some form of statement.
8	Make sure each action in your strategic plan: 1) Starts with a verb. 2) Can be assigned to someone to undertake. 3) Can be completed by a certain date.

Failing to Follow a Stakeholder Structure

Inner Logic Item 1 is: Make sure your strategic plan follows a key stakeholder structure; otherwise, it's likely to become an operational plan.

In an earlier chapter, we've already encountered the US Securities and Exchange Commission (SEC). Its *Strategic Plan* is 59 pages long. This was prepared in accordance with the Government Performance and Results Act 1993. At the time this plan was published, the agency had 4,100 staff.

Make sure your strategic plan follows a key stakeholder structure; otherwise, it's likely to become an operational plan.

The plan describes the SEC's job as monitoring and regulating the securities industry. It states:

> Following the stock market crash of 1929, Congress passed the Securities Act of 1933 and the Securities Exchange Act of 1934, which established the Securities and Exchange Commission to enforce the new securities laws, promote stability in the markets, and to protect investors. Two concepts pervade both Acts: Companies offering their stock to the public must disclose the truth about their business, the securities they are selling, and the risks involved in investing. People who sell and trade securities – brokers, dealers, and exchanges – must treat investors fairly and honestly, putting investors' interests first.[1]

Within these statements, we can see the emergence of the SEC's key stakeholders: Investors, Companies Offering Stock, Brokers, Dealers, Exchanges, the General Public and Government-as-Owner (of the SEC) – to name those that stand out. Following this, we might expect the SEC to develop its strategies and consequent actions around these groups – thus taking an outside-in view of what it does. I've experienced numerous times that this approach pushes a management team to places its members find uncomfortable. Frequently, they have to admit that they don't know what their key stakeholders really want. If strategic planning doesn't produce discomfort in a management team and board, it's not strategic planning. It's probably business as usual.

The SEC tells us how it developed its plan – its "strategic planning process," as it labels it. This involved "a team of senior managers and staff began formulating the agency's strategic plan. The team, comprised of representatives from 16 of the SEC's divisions and offices, possesses extensive knowledge of the SEC's programs and major initiatives. In developing the strategic plan, the team considered and discussed the condition of domestic and international securities markets, recent changes in the marketplace, legislative developments, and issues affecting investors and the general public. Organizational considerations such as human capital, diversity management, financial resources, and technology were also evaluated."[2]

As I've said, when a management team gets together, it often looks in on itself, writing down what it and other members of the organization do.

The SEC appears to have done just that. The plan is organized around four "goals": "Goal 1 – Enforce Compliance with Federal Securities Laws"; "Goal 2 – Sustain an Effective and Flexible Regulatory Environment"; "Goal 3 – Encourage and Promote Informed Investment Decision-Making"; "Goal 4 – Maximize the Use of SEC Resources." Further reading suggests that this is a *strategic plan without true strategies*. In particular, the "Strategies" sub-section contains a further four action-type statements that are not strategies.[3] What's important to note here is that the plan's content has been driven by its initial structure.

Failing to Create a Stakeholder-Based Strategy

Inner Logic Item 2 is: Make sure the key stakeholder structure you have identified isn't violated during the process of developing the strategies in your plan.

Let me turn to a company I'll call Diversified, which I assisted to develop the strategic plans of its five divisions. Diversified operates in the Asia-Pacific region, with more than 2,500 employees and sales of over $250 million. It is made up of five operating divisions and corporate services. The divisions are all very different: Shipping, Manufacturing, Hotels, Transport and Property. Following workshops I conducted for the company, each division developed its individual strategic plan, which sat within Diversified's corporate planning document. As usual, I had them design their strategic plans by identifying their key stakeholders.

Make sure that the key stakeholder structure you have identified isn't violated during the process of developing the strategies in your plan.

I was asked by the CEO to review each division's strategic plan and did so, about 18 months after my initial involvement. I ran a Strategic Plan Check-Up Workshop for each division's management team. While each division's plans had been reviewed by Head Office executives every quarter and updated by each division's management team – introducing any needed changes and checking on implementation progress – my workshop was an opportunity for a complete external review.

In the case of one division, Shipping, here's what I found. ("CEO" refers to the head of Diversified as a whole, not the division's general manager.) In the period since my initial workshops, the division's management team had introduced a logical flaw. It occurred in the section where objectives and strategy are written under one of the stakeholders, "CEO/Shareholders."

Here the plan had turned feral, adding to the original list a new stakeholder that was internal to the division. This was "Business Units," which referred to the units within the Shipping Division. Business units *within* a division cannot be key stakeholders *of* the division itself.

When I looked at the objectives management had set for those units, it was clear that they belonged with another of the division's key stakeholders, i.e., Customers. On closer examination, I realized that nearly all of the strategies, actions and associated objectives for "Business Units" should be transferred to Customers. All these statements had to be re-written in the light of this re-focus, but it produced a much clearer and improved strategic plan. Market research wouldn't have helped here; it was a question of inner logic.

Developing Unmeasurable Objectives

Inner Logic Item 3 is: Make sure the organization objectives in your strategic plan are based on your key stakeholders and are consistent and measurable.

Typically, as we know from Chapter 4, a management team produces an agreed list of objectives after some to-ing and fro-ing. Here's an example of what emerged in one case: the 12 objectives came from the senior management team of a large electricity generator.

- "To create and capitalize on opportunities which improve business value."
- "To achieve a comprehensive corporate governance environment that protects and enhances the company's business value."
- "To achieve a long-term sustainable revenue stream."
- "To achieve a coal supply that meets customers' expectations."
- "To ensure sufficient overburden and interseam materials are removed to maintain adequate coal reserves."
- "To balance long-term plant performance requirements while optimizing predictability and expenditure levels to meet business needs."
- "To meet our environmental obligations and ensure outcomes favorable to the company's business position."
- "To maintain a safe and healthy work environment."
- "To ensure the company's human resources meet the future needs of the business."
- "To achieve stakeholder understanding of the company's business objectives."
- "To effectively manage the company's financial resources and optimize the allocation of available funds to achieve business success."
- "To achieve effective and efficient business support functions."

The electricity generator's strategic plan then displayed several "strategies" under *each* objective. The highest number of strategies for a single objective was six, the lowest was one. In all, 46 "strategies" were listed.

Make sure that the organization objectives in your strategic plan are based on your key stakeholders and are consistent and measurable.

The problem with this approach is twofold. Firstly, the objectives themselves are inconsistent. Some relate to a desired end state, e.g., "To achieve effective and efficient business support functions," while others read like actions, e.g., "To create and capitalize on opportunities which improve business value." There's clearly an inner-logic problem here.

Secondly, the objectives aren't measured and, in their current form, probably aren't measurable. Lacking a stakeholder structure, the plan has induced management to produce a bizarre outcome – which is not uncommon. It has come up with a set of objectives for which targets have not been set, and it has then designed strategies to achieve these untargeted results! Strategies have been produced in a vacuum.

Setting objectives and designing targets should have been based on what the electricity generator wants from each key stakeholder, e.g., profitable revenue from customers; supplies in full, on time and within specifications from suppliers; productivity and innovation from employees; and invested capital from owners. This method would have produced a well-defined set of measurable objectives and clear strategy, the outcomes of which could be monitored.

Producing Slippage in Measures

Inner Logic Item 4 is: Make sure the measures developed for an objective actually relate to that objective and cover it comprehensively.

Care must be taken to remain consistent in designing measures for objectives. Slippage can easily occur between developing the objectives themselves and designing the measures appropriate for those objectives. The strategic plan of the Property Division of Diversified provides a case in point.

Make sure that the measures developed for an objective relate to that objective and cover it comprehensively.

While this division structured its objectives according to its key stakeholders, it failed to remain consistent in the objective-to-measure process.

Take the instance of the objective for employees: "To increase productivity, accuracy and attendance." The four measures listed for this objective were: "$ revenue/employee," "% absenteeism," "# hours spent on training," and "% of employees competent to do their jobs." (Note that the *style* of the measures themselves does follow that outlined in a previous chapter.)

The first two of these are fine as they relate to elements in the objective itself – "productivity" and "attendance." But the third and fourth measures do not belong with this objective because they are not measures of productivity, accuracy or attendance. This is *slippage*, and it's common. What's also noticeable is that the "accuracy" objective hasn't been measured at all – another form of slippage. I see these problems frequently in strategic plans. To avoid it, management teams must be forever watchful for inner-logic issues.

Designing "Strategy" That Isn't

Inner Logic Item 5 is: Make sure the strategic factors you have identified for your key stakeholders are from their perspective, outside-in.

Influencing key stakeholders' decisions so that they benefit your entity is what your strategies are all about. Consequently, accurately identifying these stakeholders' decision criteria, i.e., strategic factors, is crucial to the effectiveness of any strategic plan.

Make sure that the strategic factors you have identified for your key stakeholders are from their perspective, outside-in.

Let me return briefly to that very familiar business, the convenience store. Picture this: you're driving home from work, and you wish to buy a few items. How do you choose one convenience store over another? I've asked this question dozens of times in my seminars, and the answers invariably are: location (not on a busy road, easy parking, etc.), hours of operation (it's open), store presentation (well laid out, clean, tidy), range of goods sold (it has what I want), customer service (pleasant and informative staff) and price (not necessarily the cheapest, but reasonable). Any strategy for a convenience store's *customers* must be based on effective performance on these factors and, if the store wants to achieve a competitive advantage – as it surely would – doing better than the competition on one or more of them.

Let's now look more closely at this process and how it obeyed the principles of inner logic. 1) We put ourselves in the shoes of a typical convenience-store customer, which wasn't hard, and looked at the store from that perspective: outside, looking in. 2) We remained true to this sound perspective throughout the list; we didn't change perspectives halfway through. These are important but frequently overlooked requirements of developing strategy effectively. If we look again at the strategic plan of the Shipping Division of Diversified, we can note the violation of these principles.

The management team of Shipping, based on its knowledge and experience, identified and defined the following seven items as "strategic factors" for its customers: customer service (simple transactions, speed in reacting to requests, providing information, dealing with complaints), quality (delivery of orders in-full and on-time, no damage, duty of care, accurate invoicing and statements), service range (effective coverage of needs, ship capacity and frequency), trading terms (favorable conditions, available credit), price (reasonable amount paid for services), sales and marketing (information gathering, reporting and communicating competitive activity and commercial opportunities), and financial resources (capacity, company reputation, commercial orientation). The management team then developed strategies based on these factors and placed them in the division's strategic plan.

Now I don't need market research to tell me that part of the division's list of strategic factors is *wrong*. If I put myself in the shoes of the Shipping Division's customers, as you and I did in the case of the convenience store, only five of these factors ring true: customer service, quality, service range, trading terms and price. As a customer of Shipping, "sales and marketing" is *not* a strategic factor that I would nominate. It is an *activity* of Shipping. The seventh item, "financial resources," is also *not* a strategic factor for Shipping's customers. They couldn't care less about the Shipping Division's financial resources. They're concerned about the outcome for them. In developing the list of strategic factors, Shipping's management needed to be consistent and not shift its perspective to inside-out. This inner logic slip led the team to shift from true strategic factors to descriptions of activity.

Writing the Wrong Definitions

Inner Logic Item 6 is: Make sure the definitions of strategic factors are those of key stakeholders, not those of management.

Nominating the strategic factors for a key stakeholder is one thing; getting the definitions right is another. Take "customer service" for Shipping above. Its definition is "simple transactions, speed in reacting to requests, providing information, dealing with complaints." The definition is based on the management team's extensive knowledge of the industry and its customers' needs. But what if an essential element, such as assisting with technical advice, is missing? That is likely to skew any strategy based on this factor.

Make sure that the definitions of strategic factors are those of key stakeholders, not those of management.

In fine-tuning a definition of customer service, there's no substitute for talking to customers. In my experience, a few well-chosen interviews can yield huge dividends. But in other cases, more than fine-tuning is needed because the definitions are just plain *wrong*.

Take the strategic plan of the Manufacturing Division in Diversified. Its management team identified a set of strategic factors for one of its key stakeholders: consumers, that is, individuals who buy the division's products via retail stores. These products include ice cream and related freezer/dairy products, vegetable oils, condiments and seasonings, and health- and beauty-care products. One of the strategic factors for consumers, i.e., end users, was "quality." Whilst that's fine, its definition wasn't: "maintain brand loyalty." Brand loyalty is what the Division wants because of achieving effective quality. It's not a definition of quality from a consumer's perspective. I see this mistake often. It demonstrates yet again how difficult it is for a management team to maintain an outside-in view of what it does. Managers really struggle to shift to a different mindset and thus fail on inner logic.

Misstating Strategy

Inner Logic Item 7 is: Make sure your strategies aren't actions or some form of statement.

One of the strategic factors that Diversified's Manufacturing Division team identified for its customers was "product range." By "customers," they mean the retail stores that stock their products, while "consumers" refers to the end users, the retail stores' customers. The definition of product range was "variety of products supplied." However, when it came to writing strategy based on this factor, the team got itself into knots and ended up with a statement that was neither a strategy nor an action. In fact, it took on many of the attributes of an objective. It was: "Increase category mix to fully utilize container volumes."

Make sure that your strategies aren't actions or some form of statement.

Another example comes from the previously encountered SEC Strategic Plan. It lists four "key strategies [which] are employed across all programs."[4] Here are two: "Applying technology to enhance the operational effectiveness of the agency and to improve public access to SEC filings and other information" and "Sustaining and improving organizational excellence." They're not strategies, nor are they objectives, and they're not actions either! They're simply descriptions of what should happen in the organization – activity.

Still another example concerns the electricity-generating organization I referred to previously. Its 46 "strategies" were clearly actions. Here's one to illustrate the point: "Investigate opportunities for horizontal/vertical integration."

Returning, though, to the case of the Manufacturing Division of Diversified, I could tell from reading the actions associated with their so-called "strategy" – "increase category mix to fully utilize container volumes" – that what they really wanted to describe as their position on product range was: "Include new products that complement our existing range and fully utilize container volumes." This *is* a strategy since it describes a *position* on a strategic factor for the division.

Recording Fake Actions

Inner Logic Item 8 is: Make sure each action in your strategic plan: 1) Starts with a verb. 2) Can be assigned to someone to undertake. 3) Can be completed by a certain date.

Compared to writing strategy, writing action is easy. But even here, there are pitfalls. As an example, take a look at this "action" found in the strategic plan of Diversified's Transport Division: "Annual wage and salary review based on skill and value rating, and benchmarking." It was related to the strategic factor "rewards and recognition" for employees. The problem is that it isn't an action. This kind of "action" helps to explain why strategic plans are so poorly executed.

Make sure each action in your strategic plan: 1) Starts with a verb. 2) Can be assigned to someone to undertake. 3) Can be completed by a certain date.

As you know from an earlier chapter, actions start with a verb. Of course, not all statements that start with a verb are actions. However, Transport's "action" doesn't get to first base – it doesn't even start with a verb. What the management team wanted to say was: Establish a system for annual wage and salary review based on skill and value ratings for individuals, as well as on benchmarking pay rates against other organizations. Now *that* is an action.

As another "action" example that fails the test, take this one from Diversified's Hotels Division concerning its customers: "Establish the hotel's brand differential." It does start with a verb, but it's too broad and too vague – not an action. Or another from the same Division with the community as the key stakeholder: "Using the criterion that the company benefits from improved image perception; the company has identified the following sponsorship programs..." There's no action here, yet the General Manager and his team signed off on it. Or this one from Diversified's Property Division concerning Tenants: "Improve customer service to eliminate negative feedback." It passes one of the three elements of Inner Logic Item 8, i.e., it starts with a verb, but again it can't be assigned to an individual to undertake, nor can it have a completion date. So, it's not an action.

Improving Your Performance via Inner Logic

Market Research Has Its Place. With all its interviews, surveys, focus groups and data gathering, market research entails learning about your organization from others. Informal opinion-seeking and networking are also ways of gathering information. The techniques used and their application to strategy are highly developed and regularly applied in business. Don't conclude from this chapter that I see no value in this line of activity. I do, and I'm a strong advocate of "talking to the customer." What I do suggest, though, is that before you dash off to employ a market research company to help you, take time to sit back and consider the consistency of what you've written. This will pay huge dividends.

Apply Inner Logic. Testing inner logic requires you to examine what your management team and board design in your strategic plan and then test its validity *without reverting to external forms of data gathering*. These tests may show that you can drive trucks through the logical flaws, disconnects, inconsistencies and plain omissions that crop up in your strategic plan. These logical flaws will impact how you and your management team think, view the world and ultimately take action. Thus, attending to them is a fundamental first step to obtaining clarity of purpose and decisiveness of action and, ultimately, to boosting your organization's performance.

I find it both interesting and economical to pre-test a strategic plan based on its inner logic. I say "pre-test" because, at this point, it hasn't been implemented.

Notes

1 United States Securities and Exchange Commission, 2004. *2004–2009 Strategic Plan*. Washington: SEC, p. 5.
2 Ibid., p. 28.
3 Ibid., p. 24.
4 Ibid.

Chapter 9

Strategy Hacks
Effective Tools for Defining Strategy

As you know from Chapter 1, I have been CEO of a company that made trusses and frames for houses. It was failing when I came on board. My role was to lead the management team in turning the business around. The question we asked was: What do we need to do to lift the company's performance? And it worked. We did turn the company around.

As I now witness among my clients, this is the very same question that executive teams commonly ask in developing their strategic plans. But in strategy terms, this is the wrong question to ask. That's right – even though this was the right question for my failing truss company, it's the wrong question for effective strategy design.

By asking, "What do we need to do?" our focus drifted naturally to action. As a result, we did many things. For instance, we closed the milling operation, which cut long and large pieces of timber into smaller sections. The mill wasn't profitable. We reduced the stock levels in a bloated warehouse that contained timber mouldings for which there was little demand. We auctioned off excess equipment that had lain idle for years.

In the end, as I've said, we scraped back into a profit position. But I recognized that saving a company and building a company are two very different things. None of our actions was going to grow the company long term. The question we asked is completely wrong when it comes to designing business strategy.

I recognized that saving a company and building a company are two very different things.

Ok so, "What do we need to do?" was the wrong question. Should we then have asked: "What's our strategy?" It sounds reasonable, but in fact, this is the second question that leads people down a strategy dead end. Mentioning the word "strategy" in the question does little to clarify but much to confuse. Individual executives come up with all sorts of suggestions in reply.

DOI: 10.4324/9781003394976-10

One cluster of responses involves what we might call goals, e.g., "to be the employer of choice" or "to be number one in the industry." "That's our strategy," my clients say. Well, no, it isn't. It isn't even strategy. Another cluster involves quite specific targets, e.g., "to grow market share to 25 per cent" or "achieve an ROI (return on investment) of 15 per cent." Again, not strategy.

Another group of replies involves improvement in ongoing activity, e.g., "better training of staff" or "more expenditure on R&D (research and development)." What can I say? A fourth set of results involves good old actions, something an individual might do, e.g., "launch two new services each year" or "employ social media as part of our marketing campaigns." Again, not business strategy.

So, we commonly ask, "What do we need to do?" or "What is our strategy?" Neither tends to end up in developing an effective strategy. What sits below these two questions that leads managers down the wrong path?

By asking, "What do we need to do?" you've thrust yourself at the individual "level of analysis." The two fundamental levels, when it comes to strategic planning, are the individual and organization levels. Action occurs at the individual level. So, when managers ask, "What do we need to do?" in seeking strategy solutions, they end up focusing on the individual level when their focus should be corporate.

What about the question: "What's our strategy?" Here the underpinning problem is mainly definitional. Participants are confused about what strategy is, and the question doesn't help to clarify it. Business strategy is about positioning – of the organization. It's not about actions (by individuals), nor organization goals, nor targets, nor descriptions of activity.

The One Question That Will Get You to Strategy

As a management consultant to organizations, there is one golden question I use to focus my clients' thinking on strategy.

The question I ask is this: "As an organization, where do you stand on [strategic factor]." The strategic factor in question will depend on the key stakeholder in focus. In the case of customers of a retail store, strategic factors include customer service, range of goods sold, location, hours of operation, store presentation and price. In the case of its employees, the strategic factors include pay, recognition, organization culture, promotional prospects and type of work.

The question I ask is this: "As an organization, where do you stand on [strategic factor]."

Note the emphasis here on "as an organization." I've found that posing the question this way with clients induces managers to think outside-in. In most cases, they haven't clearly articulated their strategic positions before. They've either been assumed, or the organization has simply drifted along. So, when I ask this question, it usually cuts through like a knife. It startles. I can see the result on executives' faces: "We haven't got this sorted out."

As the responses come in, I frequently need to pull managers up as they fall into, again, describing what they're going to do. "No, no," I need to remind them, "as an organization, where do you need to stand?"

In the case of a German company that supplies specialized air-conditioning units for IT installations, the answer on the strategic factor "customer experience" was fresh: "Exceptional service pre- and post-sale and consistent service between states. A benchmark in the industry. Be a trusted advisor and knowledge leader." Note here how this isn't a goal, target, activity or action – but an organization position. The company came to this statement through extensive discussion with customers about what they wanted from a leading company in the industry. It was adopted by the organization because the strategic planning team recognized that it would drive results on their objective to increase profitable revenue.

As another example, take the case of one of Australia's budget airlines, Jetstar. Its position on price is: "Find a lower comparable price online, and we'll beat it by 10 per cent." Jetstar's management has figured that adopting this price position will capture a giant slice of the low-price market, thus driving sales.

Ideas about action and activity tend to dominate when the focus is on business strategy. To escape this bias, an organization's performance must be viewed outside-in. You arrive at that perspective only by asking the right question.

Ideas about action and activity tend to dominate when the focus is on business strategy.

Forget Market Timing, Focus on Point of Difference

Another red herring that catches many leaders is fretting over market timing. We live in an age of great innovation spurred by amazing advances in information technology, the internet and social media. These changes are inspiring a constant stream of new business ideas. However, many of these ideas will be snuffed out in their prime. The reason? Clumsy thinking expressed as: "It's been done before" or "You're too late; someone's already thought of it."

The tragedy is that market timing is rarely the issue nor the impediment it's made out to be. The solution in most cases is to ignore the timing question and instead aim for an answer to: "What's your point of difference?" See, for example, Exhibit 9.1.

The tragedy is that market timing is rarely the issue nor the impediment it's made out to be.

Exhibit 9.1   Leveraging Advantage

Eric is the CEO of an online business success story. It sells books and is a competitor to Amazon. I'll call it Livre. Today it's a healthy, profitable company with nearly 300 staff and sales in the millions of dollars. It rose from humble beginnings about 15 years ago. Like many start-ups, it was greeted with the all-too-familiar timing pronouncement. As Eric put it, "We were told that we started too late in online bookselling."

But he was not deflected by comments like this; instead, he pressed on, looking for a point of difference at every turn. The first of these concerned product range. This became the thin edge of the wedge for future success.

At this stage of the market's development, the bricks-and-mortar booksellers were resistant to carrying some emerging genres. The traditional booksellers could see these categories were popular, but they didn't want to stock them either because they didn't think they were "good books" or because they had a distaste for fan-based genres. One example was Manga graphic novels – a niche category not to everyone's taste and not stocked by most booksellers, but one with a loyal and growing audience.

The failure of existing booksellers to fill the product-range gap provided Eric and his team with just the opening they were seeking. As a start-up eager for any sales whatsoever, they had no qualms about pouncing on each opportunity.

Livre clawed its way into the market and then provided better service online. At the time, the bookshops were developing an online sales presence through their websites. But their moves were tentative at best. They were hampered by their legacy businesses, a lack of technological nous and their conservative attitudes to certain book categories. In addition, the nation's largest retail bookseller was hampered in moving with the times because it operated through a complex and cumbersome arrangement with its franchisees. In Eric's view, this company should have occupied the market space that Livre now does, but Eric played his advantage.

Having established product range as a starting point of difference, Livre dug in, expanding its range to other genres with sales potential. It took on more conventional books and added the supply of books to the nation's universities and colleges and to large corporate accounts.

Eric sums up the company's journey this way. "What we've done over the years is to constantly look for a point of difference. This is not just any point of difference but one that customers value – and that's an important distinction. They want a suitable product range, and we monitor that closely. They want speedy delivery, we're great at that. They want to know how far away their order is, and we have the best order tracking in the business. They want to be able to talk to someone locally and not get the run-around, and we've spent a lot of money on our local call center."

Livre has come out ahead by outdoing the competition on value calculated by weighing up the strategic factors relevant to customers – brand, delivery speed, order accuracy, customer service, product range and delivered book price.

I've had a personal experience with this. In my mid-twenties, I had a promising business idea to produce cladding for multi-story buildings in Australia under license to a Norwegian company. The product was unavailable locally. But I was young, and I sought advice from someone with much more industry experience. He said, "There are a lot of makers of cladding out there." Despite a strong point of difference – it was made from innovative materials – I listened and dropped the idea. A few years later, the same person shared this with me. "You'd have made a lot of money if you'd gone ahead with that idea."

Misguided advice like this and subsequent project abandonment represents a considerable loss at the personal, business, industry and national levels.

I recently sat with a client called Jane, who wanted to discuss her new business idea. She had a couple of decades in business-to-business sales experience and found herself out of work through COVID. Her start-up idea was sales training and coaching. If you're like me, your visceral reaction is something like, "There's a lot of competition out there." Jane had heard this from many sources.

However, rather than dismissing the idea as a stupid folly, we set to work focusing on her point of difference. And, over a couple of hours and a few cups of coffee, a real and distinctive point of departure emerged, including focusing on women business owners.

You can be quite certain that the founders of Google, Larry Page and Sergey Brin, received the "it's-been-done-before" message along their business journey. The Google search tool was preceded by many others, including Yahoo!, Magellan, Lycos, Infoseek and Excite. But Page and Brin pressed on, confident they had a point of difference that mattered to customers. Google has succeeded when previous search engines haven't because its internet tool has performed better in ways important to customers – such as speed, relevance and accuracy.

In Strategy, It's Ok to Say, "We Don't Know"

Not knowing is unacceptable in some occupations. If you were to pop your head into the pilot's cabin before take-off on your next flight and ask, "Do you know how to fly this thing?" you're not expecting to hear, "No, we don't know." That would have you backing hastily to the exit. Knowing is highly valued and, in this case, very important – to passenger safety.

But flying a plane, operating a piece of machinery or undertaking brain surgery are vastly different from guiding an organization into its future. In business strategy, you're confronted not only with known unknowns, but also unknown unknowns.

In business strategy, you're confronted not only with known unknowns, but also unknown unknowns.

You might think personal humility is an odd starting point on the journey to corporate competitive advantage. But this is exactly where you must begin if you are to navigate your business successfully in today's environment.

If the culture of your executive team does not accept "we don't know," you have a problem. Going forward from there in this fast-moving world can only lead to further issues. To overcome this, organizations are turning to openness.

If the culture of your executive team does not accept "we don't know," you have a problem.

It's impossible for boards and executive teams to have all the answers. Consequently, many strategic conclusions they make are outdated or just plain wrong.

When Satya Nadella took over as CEO of Microsoft, after 14 years under Steve Ballmer's reign, the signs were there that the business had begun to ossify. It needed a strategic shift to keep pace with rapidly changing circumstances and devouring competitors.

As Nadella observed, Microsoft had become a company of "know-it-alls." So, he set about converting the company into one in which its managers were "learn-it-alls." One of the principles driving this was the need "to be insatiable in our desire to learn from the outside and bring that learning into Microsoft." [1] That required executives to admit "we don't know."

DHL is another company whose executives are prepared to admit "we don't know" when it comes to strategy. It operates four "innovation centers" in Singapore, Bonn, Dubai and Chicago. These are set up to engage customers in uncovering "emerging trends," generating "insights" and identifying "competitive services." As the company explains: "We welcome customers, partners, and other innovative thinkers to engage with DHL experts."

Lego, too, has used this logic to its advantage through Lego Ideas. The company asks its followers and users to contribute suggestions in "contests" via its website. Ideas go through an initial intake, expert review, crowd vote and winner announcement. Of course, this operates on a grand scale, but is it unrealistic that you might engage a section of your key stakeholders in cracking a strategy puzzle that relates to them?

Research has shown that the further away you are from a problem in terms of technical expertise, the more likely you are to come up with a "winning solution." Your ideas are less likely to be grounded in the everyday and to have become staid. That's important to recall. Translated into generating strategic options, this means that downing tools and admitting "we don't know" might be the best strategic idea on your road to success.

Research has shown that the further away you are from a problem in terms of technical expertise, the more likely you are to come up with a "winning solution."

Your biggest barrier to strategy's "we don't know" is your organization's culture. As Satya Nadella found at Microsoft, attitudes and behavior become embedded and habitual. Just as Microsoft demonstrated, change must start at the top. With that as a given, here are two suggestions to overcome your team's strategy blind spots – one in-person and one remote.

The in-person step involves strategy co-creation. This requires you to invite members of your key stakeholder groups to sit with your executives and other staff in workshops. The aim of working together is to generate ideas about where your organization or business unit might head. In the case of employees, this isn't so difficult, and to some extent, you may already be doing this. With direct customers and end users, this may be a bigger step. But it's doable.

Remember, outside involvement can go beyond your immediate stakeholders, taking in participants outside your industry. Those distant from your industry will approach your questions with fresh eyes.

The remote step involves crowdsourcing for strategy insights. Think about it. Customers and other key stakeholders are only too happy to offer their opinions. After all, if you listen, they benefit. Even for a small business, this is achievable. The technology is there and accessible, e.g., Openideo, Innocentive and UTest.

Improve Strategy Execution with Artificial Intelligence

Strategy execution has always been tricky. Volumes have been written over decades about how to do it. An equal quantity of material has been generated on why strategy execution is so poor. One recent report, for example, adds to the string of statistics finding that only about "one-fifth of organizations achieve 80% or more of their strategic targets."[2]

It's time to acknowledge one thing – CEOs and their organizations have failed. It's not through a lack of trying, though. The problem is that turning intention in a strategic plan into action at the frontline is extremely complex. And when we face a difficult problem, we humans have always turned to one thing – technology. The computer on which I'm working is a clear illustration of that.

Artificial intelligence (AI) is the newest frontier of technology, and it offers huge potential to solve our problems in strategy execution. While AI has been around for some time, its modern reincarnation is driven by the advent of massive computer power.

Let's look at AI's potential to help you deal with two issues in the strategy execution space – coordination and customization.

Organizations are structured along functional lines for efficiency. And it works. Putting experts in accounting together, for instance, pools their knowledge, leads to economies of scale, and speeds up processing. But when it comes to strategy delivery, these functional seams turn into handicaps.

This is because specialized departments collect and corral data specific to their function and don't share it, e.g., marketing stores data on customer satisfaction and buying habits, HR stores data on employee engagement and employee turnover, finance stores data on customer and employee costs.

Customers, on the other hand, are outside and want a seamless experience which the internal functional structure is not designed to achieve.

An organization that is employing AI to address this issue is Australia's Woolworths. The retailer is one of the nation's two largest supermarket chains, with around 10 million customers. To obtain a competitive edge, Woolworths' management has moved towards examining its departmental data in a holistic way. It's achieving this via what it calls an "enterprise data lake," which pools data from several functions, e.g., Sales, Marketing and Finance.

This is helping Woolworths' senior management unlock departmental data for more effective strategy execution. Angelo Clayton, Woolworths' General Manager for IT explains: "Part of [the] challenge was the data literally sat in so many different places within the organisation. Each business unit built its siloed data warehouse, and it was really just impossible to be able to bring all that data together in a trusted and reliable fashion."[3]

Applying AI to the pooling of departmental information is helping Woolworths allocate resources across its 1,051 supermarkets far more effectively to achieve a better customer experience. This includes much better localization of the products stocked in each store.

Consumers want to be treated as individuals – to be understood and appreciated. Yet organizations are growing bigger and less personal to achieve economies of scale and lower prices. The shift from the local corner store, where you knew the owner, and he or she knew you, to large supermarkets with high staff turnover is one illustration. This is happening in banking too.

Consumers want to be treated as individuals – to be understood and appreciated.

One organization tackling this is the Commonwealth Bank, Australia's largest, with more than 10 million personal and small business customers. The bank is investing $5 billion over the next five years in AI. This will help the bank customize its offerings to customers and provide it with a competitive edge.

The bank's General Manager of Customer Decisioning, Dr. Andrew McMullan, explains. "Every time a customer goes into NetBank [the bank's online banking system], uses the app, calls us, goes to a branch, that calls our Customer Engagement Engine." This then triggers the opportunity to finesse the bank's service and products for each individual customer.

For example, if a customer walks into a bank branch and presents his or her card, the bank teller will receive an instant computerized prompt that he or she used the app to investigate car loans. Staff can follow up by offering related loan products or services. The bank refers to this as the "next best conversation."

Strategy Hacks for Your Business

While every business is different, these strategy hacks apply to all kinds of organizations, whether you're a multinational, a small business or a not-for-profit.

Take a Stand on Your Strategic Factors. Don't get led astray by questions such as "What do we need to do?" or "What's our strategy?" These are not effective ways to get you to where you need to go, which is to take a position on the strategic factors that matter to your stakeholders. The key question to ask is therefore "*As an organization,* where do you stand on [strategic factor]."

Point of Difference Is More Important Than Timing. Whether you're a start-up entrepreneur or a director of a large multinational, you need to be wary of the timing myth. It's destructive to personal morale and crippling to organizational culture. It can also be expensive in terms of missed opportunities. A single throwaway line like "it's been done before" can dampen initiative and burn out innovation.

Whether you're a start-up entrepreneur or a director of a large multinational, you need to be wary of the timing myth.

No matter your business idea, the golden rule of business success will always apply – outperform the competition on the strategic factors that matter to customers, and you'll succeed.

Humility Trumps Hubris. Intended or not, your business has a way of putting pressure on its managers. Pressure to get results. Pressure to meet targets. And, worst of all, pressure to "know." Ego, hubris and saving face get wrapped up in this and the mindset becomes "I can't admit I don't know." The result? Your organization closes in on itself in the pursuit of answers. To avoid this, find an opportunity to discuss personal humility at your next strategy meeting. It could be your business's gateway to truly effective strategy.

AI Opens Execution Opportunities. You will no doubt have witnessed that the struggle with strategy execution has been going on for an awfully long time. You'll also be aware that there is no shortage of remedies proposed to tackle it. These include using cross-functional teams, establishing a culture of collaboration, creating a decentralized organization structure and improving listening to customers.

While all these solutions have a place, each is subject to human frailties which show up as a limited ability to deal with complexity and achieve consistency. You may need something else to make strategy execution a success. I suggest it's time to embrace AI as a useful tool in pursuing better strategy execution.

Notes

1 Ibarra, H. & Rattan, A. 2018. Microsoft: Instilling a growth mindset. *London Business School Review*, 3: 50–53.
2 Harvard Business Review Analytic Services. 2019. *Testing organizational boundaries to improve strategy execution*. Boston: Research Report.
3 Crozier, R. 2019. How Woolworths uses Google to power its massive analytics uplift. *IT News*, April.

Chapter 10

Strategy's Code
Put the Pieces Together

Strategy is among the most overused, misused and misunderstood concepts in the management lexicon. As such, it becomes a catch-all for almost everything: a list of activities, program descriptions, goals, objectives, values and actions.[1] The list goes on.

Does it matter? I think it does – at two levels.

The first is your managers. In their bewilderment, they most likely thrash around the subject of strategy, working up a sweat – debating, discussing and disagreeing on the question: "Is that a strategy?" The result is disharmony, confusion, downright dysfunction and an awful lot of wasted time and effort. Frustration on this level is not good. It leads eventually to avoiding strategy altogether!

The second level concerns your organization. If your managers and directors don't come to grips with strategy because they can't grasp the concept, your organization will end up strategy-less and suffer the consequences. Being bereft of strategy sounds impossible, I must admit, but I regularly witness organizations that are completely operations focused. I frequently hear from managers that their organizations "lack strategy."

Without a clear and crisp understanding of the subject, your managers and directors will completely bypass this essential ingredient of success. Your organization's success will be nipped in the bud, reduced to a hit-and-miss affair. If chance, luck and mere fluke become the underlying drivers of your "strategy-less" organization, you're not exactly in a great spot.

I've had the luxury of concentrating on strategy as a specialty over a long period of time. Slowly but surely, the cloud that existed over it has lifted, and clarity has emerged. Putting the pieces together has produced a system, the Strategic Factor System.[2] Exhibit 10.1 summarizes the essential elements of strategy's code. Employ this framework to drive your organization to sustained success.

DOI: 10.4324/9781003394976-11

Exhibit 10.1   Strategy's Code[3]

Strategy
- Strategy is the way an organization achieves competitive advantage.[4]
- A strategy is a position taken by an organization on a strategic factor that achieves an objective.
- A strategy is designed to:
  - meet a stakeholder's expectations and
  - exceed a competitor's performance.
- Strategy is an organization-level concept.

Action
- Action is what an individual does.
- Action is not strategy.
- Organizations don't act, they take positions.
- Action is an individual-level concept.

Stakeholders
- Successful strategy relies on identifying an organization's key stakeholders.
- Key stakeholders are those organizations, groups and individuals with whom an organization interacts and on whom it depends for success.
- Targeting stakeholders within a stakeholder category is essential for success.

Strategic Factors
- Strategic factors are derived from stakeholders.
- Strategic factors are based on what stakeholders want *from* an organization.
- Strategic factors are the criteria stakeholders employ to assess an organization's performance.

Organization Objectives
- Organization objectives shape strategy.
- Organization objectives, like strategies, are classified according to key stakeholders.
- Organization objectives are based on what an organization wants *from* a key stakeholder.

Notes

1 Richard Rumelt also makes this point in Rumelt, R. 2011. *Good strategy, bad strategy*. New York: Crown Business.
2 First detailed in book form in Kenny, G. 2001. *Strategic factors: Develop and measure winning strategy*. Sydney: President Press. Re-published in 2005 by Elsevier Butterworth-Heinemann as *Strategic planning and performance management*.
3 These statements are made in the context of an organization's strategic plan. Individuals may have their own personal strategic plan. In which case they would develop strategy for themselves.
4 These statements refer to "organization," but they apply equally well to any business unit that requires a strategic plan.

Glossary

Listed here are the major terms employed in this book, which are also used in our Strategic Factor System. We try to keep terms to a minimum. The definitions are based on our experience working with various organizations and industries.

Action plan A list of actions that need to be undertaken to execute strategy. An action plan states what is to be done, who is to do it and when it is to be completed.

Behavioral outcome A statement that describes what an organization or business unit wants a key stakeholder to do.

Competitive advantage The extent to which an organization or business unit delivers value superior to its competitors.

Differentiation How an organization or business unit distinguishes itself on strategic factors.

Diversification The extent to which the activities of an organization or business unit are spread across industries.

Industry The environment of an organization or business unit, composed of a set of customers, suppliers, competitors, etc.

Industry segment Part of an industry.

Key performance indicators (KPIs) Measures of performance that are central to success.

Key stakeholders Organizations, business units and individuals with whom an organization or business unit interacts and on whom it depends for success, e.g., customers, employees, owners and suppliers.

Measure A metric such as the number of units produced, per cent market share or dollar revenue.

Mission   A statement that answers the question, "What business are we in?"

Objectives   Statements that describe what an organization or business unit wants to achieve via its key stakeholders, e.g., to increase revenue from customers.

Operational plan   A plan that takes competitiveness as a given and develops the way it can be achieved, e.g., marketing plan, manufacturing plan.

Outcome   An end result for a key stakeholder, organization or business unit.

Performance   The outcomes achieved by an entity such as an organization. There is no performance without outcomes and no outcomes without stakeholders.

Positioning   The placement of an organization or business unit in the minds of its key stakeholders based on strategic factors.

Strategic factors   Criteria on which an organization or business unit must do well to succeed; used by stakeholders to assess performance.

Strategic Factor System   An integrated approach to identifying strategic factors, setting objectives and targets, and writing strategy and actions – all classified by key stakeholders.

Strategic plan   A plan that achieves competitive advantage for an organization or business unit.

Strategy   A statement that describes how competitive advantage is to be achieved on a strategic factor. It is a position taken by an organization on a strategic factor that achieves an objective.

Target   A level of performance on a key performance indicator that an organization or business unit sets out to achieve.

Value   What a key stakeholder gets for what it gives. It is based on a key stakeholder's assessment of results in relation to its strategic factors.

Index

Pages in *italics* refer to figures, pages in **bold** refer to tables and pages in **_bold/italics_** refer to boxes.

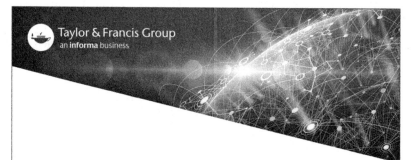

Printed in the United States
by Baker & Taylor Publisher Services